The Rockhound's Guide
to NEW MEXICO

by
Melinda Crow

Consulting Editor
W.R.C. Shedenhelm

FALCON™

Falcon Press® Publishing Co., Inc.
Helena, Montana

Falcon Press is continually expanding its list of recreational guidebooks using the same general format as this book. All books include detailed descriptions, accurate maps, and all the information necessary for enjoyable trips. You can order extra copies of this book and get information and prices for other Falcon guidebooks by writing Falcon Press, P.O. Box 1718, Helena, MT 59624. Also, please ask for a free copy of our current catalog listing all Falcon Press books.

Library of Congress Cataloging-in-Publication Data

Crow, Melinda
    The rockhound's guide to New Mexico / by Melinda Crow : consulting editor, W.R.C. Shedenhelm.
        p.   cm.
    Includes index.
    ISBN 1-56044-340-5
    1. Rocks—New Mexico—Collection and preservation—Guidebooks.
2. Minerals—New Mexico—Collection and preservation—Guidebooks.
3. New Mexico–Guidebooks. I. Shedenhelm W.R.C. II. Title.
    QE445.N6C76   1995   95-15049
    549.9789'075—dc20   CIP

 Text pages printed on recycled paper.

CAUTION

Outdoor recreation activities are by their very nature potentially hazardous. All participants in such activities must assume the responsibility for their own actions and safety. The information contained in this guidebook cannot replace sound judgement and good decision-making skills, which help reduce risk exposure, nor does the scope of this book allow for disclosure of all the potential hazards and risks involved in such activities.

Learn as much as possible about the outdoor recreation activities you participate in, prepare for the unexpected, and be safe and cautious. The reward will be a safer and more enjoyable experience.

CONTENTS

SOUTHWEST

SOUTHEAST

ACKNOWLEDGMENTS

Rockhounds tend to be just a little reserved when it comes to telling strangers the whereabouts of their favorite collecting spots. I, therefore, wish to express my deepest gratitude to those who shared information with me, even knowing that I planned to publish it in this book.

Thanks go to my dad and his wife, Bill and Louise West of Albuquerque. They not only provided room and board numerous times, but also allowed me to drag them around for miles looking for rocks. And it was always with smiles on their faces. Thanks also to Louise's family who welcomed me home to New Mexico as if I had never left.

To Chuck and Mark Hassel, my most trustworthy photography and geology advisors, I say thanks yet again. I could fill this page with sappy words of appreciation for your help, but something tells me you'd rather have cheesecake. And so you shall have it. Name your flavor. Thanks also to Cindy Hassell who is always there to provide writing inspiration and loan me her husband for his photographical genius. Cheesecake for you as well.

Final thanks go to my daughter Alyssa and my husband Gary who share in all my travels and for whom are reserved all the treasures of my heart.

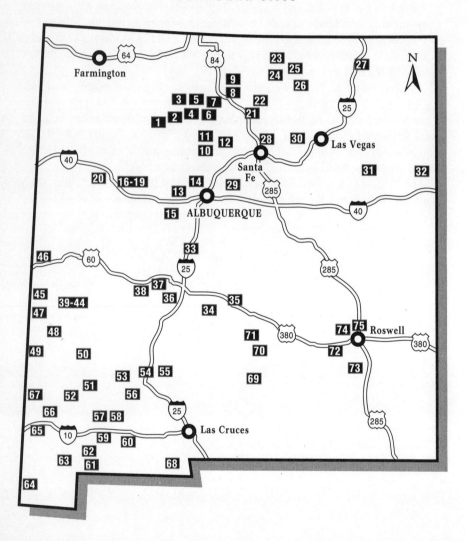

NEW MEXICO
rockhound sites

MAP LEGEND

Rockhound Site

Interstate

Paved Road

Gravel Road

Unimproved
Dirt Road

Park/Refuge/
Nat'l Forest
Boundary

Waterway

Building

Railroad Track

City

Town

Campground

Mountain Peak

888 Interstate

88 U.S. Highway

88 88 State Highway

88 County/Forest Road

Lake/Reservoir

ABOUT THIS BOOK

I had the privilege of growing up with homes in both Texas and New Mexico. I spent my summers climbing mountains, fishing in clear streams, and learning about an enchanted culture. For a flat-land kid from the Texas Panhandle, each hill and crevice was truly magical. Unfortunately, familiarity often breeds boredom. In my early adulthood, I sought greener pastures with fewer tourists, and I lost sight of the remarkable beauty I once considered my backyard.

When I began working on The Rockhound's Guide to New Mexico, it was, therefore, with ambivalence. Obviously I knew the territory, but could I do it justice? Could my eyes once again see the magic? As I wandered the state seeking its mineral treasures, I continually reminded myself to close my eyes to what they had seen before, to seek new vistas.

By viewing New Mexico from the perspective of the rockhound, I discovered my vision was clearer than ever before. I saw that the enchantment emanates from many sources: the people, the rugged deserts, the pine-covered mountains, and the rocks, magical rocks.

Use this book as your guide to the magic, but know going in that something so seductive can also be elusive. The best rocks aren't always easy to find. Because of this, the site descriptions in the guide are rated by difficulty. This rating is based on both the ease of finding the spot and finding the right stuff when you get there.

This specimen of clear, pink chalcedony was found alongside the road near Hermanas.

Some of the collecting areas found in this guide are well known. For these I sought to provide updated information regarding roads and availability of good material. New Mexico has been scoured by rockhounds for centuries, and there are many localities known for this or that. But it doesn't help to know that there's petrified wood out west of Albuquerque if you don't know which road to take. Because of this, many of the sites are designed to pinpoint ideal collecting spots.

I also tried to include a selection of sites that I call imperfects. These are places with collectibles that are slightly less than spectacular located very near commonly-known sites with near perfect specimens of something else. Site 61 is an imperfect. The chalcedony found along the road near Hermanas is beautiful, some of the best in the state. The only reason it isn't widely known is that it is very near the Baker Egg Mine where collectors come from around the world to look for outstanding thunder eggs, walking right over the chalcedony in the process.

Remember that like any enchantress, New Mexico can be hard and unforgiving. Take vehicle recommendations given in the site listings very seriously and stay alert to changing weather conditions. Read through the introductory material designed to give you an overview of the state's terrain and wildlife. Most importantly, travel prepared. Detailed maps, extra water, tow chains, and spare tires are all life-saving equipment here.

If you are new to New Mexico, open your eyes wide. See it all. The state is a living museum of culture, science, and history. Remember to tread lightly though, so the people who call the land their home will embrace your return. And for those who think they know the Land of Enchantment, come with me searching for the slivers of beauty you just might have missed.

INTRODUCTION TO NEW MEXICO

New Mexico is quiet. The people are spread across vast stretches of desert, plains, and mountain. Though it is the fifth largest state (behind Alaska, Texas, California, and Montana), it ranks thirty-sixth in population. Only 1.6 million people call the state home, and more than one-third of those live in the largest city, Albuquerque.

The state capital is Santa Fe. The state flower is Yucca, also called soapweed. Its roots make a sudsing agent when crushed and was often used for washing by Native Americans. The state tree is piñon, which means "nut pine." Piñon nuts are about the size of a coffee bean and are often roasted to bring out the flavor. The state bird is the roadrunner, which is a common sight in the lower altitudes.

Government agencies are the largest employers, but the economy is diverse, drawing from sources that include manufacturing, mining, dairy production, cattle, farming, and tourism.

More than thirty-two percent of the land in New Mexico is owned by the federal government. The land includes national forests, national parks, military

New Mexico puts on a show of ever changing landforms and weather conditions.

installations, and land managed by the BLM. Much of the cattle grazing land in the state is BLM land under lease to ranchers.

New Mexico's elevation ranges from 2,842 feet in the southeast corner to the highest tip of Wheeler Peak, which rises above Taos at a majestic 13,161 feet. In places like these the silence is broken only by the howl of the coyote or the whispering of the pines. In Chaco Canyon the silent walls of ancient cultures stand tribute to the enchantment of this peaceful place.

Geologically speaking New Mexico has been anything but quiet. Violent volcanic eruptions once thundered across the plains. Earthquakes split the ground, driving massive walls of granite skyward. Great seas crashed inland, covering the land before retreating again. A pair of north-south faults tore the state in half, allowing the Rio Grande to flow through the state from the Colorado highlands.

Rockhound Treasures

Geologic activity left in its wake a huge amount of mineralogical treasure for the rockhound to seek. Unusual mineral displays, fossils, and jasper are the primary finds in the northeast section of the state. In the northwest, look for rich black, red, and brown agate, more obsidian than one hound could ever hope to collect, petrified wood, and a few selected fossil sites. Moving south into the mining districts, collectibles range from perfect cubic fluorites at Bingham to richly-hued thunder eggs near the Mexican border. The array of material found in the state is almost mind boggling, as is the quality. Whether they come seeking micro-mount mineral specimens, gemstones, or material for cutting and polishing, rockhounds are rarely disappointed with New Mexico.

The Landscape

New Mexico is a land of surprises. It is possible to drive through green dairy country, cactus-covered desert, and snow-laden pine forests in the short space of an hour. The daily mean temperature statewide is about 56 degrees Fahrenheit. The sun shines on about seventy-six percent of the days. That percentage places New Mexico third among the other forty-nine states behind only Arizona and Nevada. Average rainfall ranges from 12 to 16 inches. The variances in elevation allow for six of the seven life zones recognized in the United States.

Summer daytime temperatures reach well into the nineties throughout most of the state, and nighttime temperatures are known to drop considerably, particularly at higher elevations. Winter brings a wide range of weather factors. Heavy snowfall blankets the mountains in the north, while the southern reaches of the state remain relatively mild. Deming and Las Cruces are winter havens for sun-lovers from the northern United States.

The northwestern corner of the state contains both the desert "badlands" surrounding Farmington and breathtaking sections of the Cibola, Santa Fe, and Carson national forests. Several peaks in the region rise above 11,000 feet, and most of the terrain lies above 5,000 feet. The Continental Divide snakes across this section from just west of Chama to just north of Quemado. Population follows the Rio Grande north and south and Interstate Highway 40 east and west. The remaining areas are very thinly populated. The bulk of the land in the region belongs to ten separate Indian reservations.

The northeastern section of the state boasts the beautiful Sangre de Cristo Range of the Rocky Mountains. Tourist and artist havens, like Santa Fe and Taos, are the population centers, but most of the mountain range is dotted with vacation cabins. East of the mountains, the land gently slopes toward the flatlands.

The Southeastern quadrant of the state is the flattest. At the far eastern edge, oil wells dot the landscape almost as thickly as the pines of the northern regions. Cattle ranching and farming also provide income in these areas. Between the population centers of Clovis, Portales, Roswell, Artesia, Hobbs, and Carlsbad lies a whole lot of nothing. The only mountainous area in the region is found on the western edge. The Sacramento and Capitan mountain ranges come together near Ruidoso. The valleys leading into both ranges provide ideal growing conditions for farmers and ranchers.

The southwestern corner of the state is an unusual blend of desert and pine-covered mountains. The contrast is often extreme. Population is widely scattered. Most towns in the region had their beginnings connected in some manner with the business of mining. It is in this section of the state that the Old West and mining history truly spring to life. Ghost towns ring with the laughter of lucky miners and down-on-their-luck gunmen. The Gila and Apache national forests collide in this rugged region. The Wilderness areas encompassed by the Gila are some of the most staggeringly beautiful found anywhere. Amazingly, though, there are signs of civilization in and around the wilderness.

NEW MEXICO ROCKHOUNDING TIPS

Because New Mexico has such a diverse array of collectibles, some thought and research should go into planning your rockhounding trips. It makes no sense to travel to Deming if your real passion is collecting mineral specimens. Likewise, a trip to the Kelly mining district could be disappointing to an agate hound. Having said that, if you have ever been interested in expanding your collecting horizons, you've come to the right place.

The sites listed in this book are categorized by material types to simplify your planning. The categories include gemstones, fossils, mineral specimens, and rocks for polishing. Additionally, if the rocks found at a site are of a size suitable only for the tumbler, that is noted.

The sites are also rated for difficulty. To aid in trip planning, both the ease of getting to the site and finding the rocks were taken into consideration. Keep in mind that in New Mexico, mileage is a very poor determination of how long it may take to reach a destination. A 60-mile drive could involve a trip across mountains on a one-lane, winding dirt road and could take several hours.

Mineral collectors seek their treasure at places like the dumps at the Kelly mine.

The maps in this book are designed to give you a simplistic reference. Traveling in New Mexico without detailed maps is asking for trouble. Forest Service maps are available in many retail outlets, or directly from the Forest Service. The BLM offers a free recreation and heritage guide that provides a quick reference to land management. For a small price they offer a more detailed version. Topographical maps are available from the U.S. Geological Survey. Addresses to write for any of the above mentioned maps are listed in the appendix of this book.

Finally, it pays to know what you're looking for. Seek out rock shops in the areas you visit. Ask them to show you examples of the local treasure. If it makes your collecting just a tad bit easier, it will be worth the stop.

NEW MEXICO WILDLIFE

Though New Mexico may be a quiet and desolate place in regard to the human population, it is teeming with other forms of life. Since rock collecting in this state often places you smack in the middle of wildlife habitats, it is a wise collector who is prepared to deal with the creatures whose homes he invades.

Snakes

Diamondback rattlesnakes are probably the most feared creature by people travelling in the western United States. The rattler can be found in all regions of New Mexico, with the greatest concentrations located at elevations below 7,000 feet. Collectors should never venture out without a snakebite kit. Know how to use it and test the suction device periodically to ensure that it works properly. Obviously the best approach would be to avoid a confrontation in the first place, so a little knowledge of the habits and lifestyles of the beast is the best defense.

Contrary to popular belief, the rattlesnake does not love extremely hot weather. In fact their levels of activity peak near 80 to 85 degrees Fahrenheit. What that means to the collector is that early morning or late evening expeditions during the warm months require extra caution. Summer daytime heat usually finds the rattler sleeping under the cover of rock ledges or brush, so care is necessary around these areas.

When spring arrives the snakes are most active. It is during this season that they must eat more to replace weight lost during winter and provide energy for mating. A word of caution regarding the young, which are born in late summer: They often are easier to provoke, less experienced at remaining undetected (making confrontations more likely), and have less control over the amount of venom injected into a bite. In other words, be particularly watchful of smaller snakes.

A walking stick about the length of a broom handle is probably the best tool for avoiding snakes. Poke and prod the brush before every step. In extremely snaky areas it is also advisable to wear heavy boots. This strategy is twofold. Boots make more noise when you walk, and they provide a tough shield between you and those fangs.

Bears

The New Mexico black bear is found in every region of the state between elevations of 5,000 and 10,000 feet. The name "black bear" is quite confusing here because the bears in this region of the country are sometimes brown. But take heart, there are no grizzlies in New Mexico, just lots of cinnamon-colored black bears.

Though there is only one species involved, there are two kinds of bears that the average traveler is likely to encounter in New Mexico. Front-country bears are those that hang out in and around populated campgrounds and towns. They come seeking food in garbage cans and often in peoples' tents. They are not generally afraid of people and sometimes appear quite tame. This segment of the bear population is steadily increasing as the tourist population increases.

Tarantulas are usually quick to get out of your way.

Back-country bears are those that range farther from population centers. They are usually quite timid in the presence of people. However, BOTH kinds are unpredictable, BOTH kinds have uncanny strength, and BOTH kinds should be avoided, if at all possible. Their habitat is usually one of dense forest or brush; the thicker the better.

Bears will eat anything. This is important to remember when camping in bear territory. They have been known to rip open tents seeking food. In mid- to late summer bears gorge themselves on wild berries and are often protective of their berry patches. Bears forage for food both day and night. Front-country bears have learned that the easiest pickings are at night. Back-country bears, however, lack the day-to-day influence of people on their feeding habits. They eat when they are hungry and sleep when they are tired, regardless of the time.

Black bears bed down either in dense brushy areas or, rarely, in trees. Unlike their cousin the grizzly, black bears do not lose their ability to climb as they mature. Black bears can climb trees with amazing speed. A mama bear will often put her cubs in trees for safety while she looks for food. For that reason it is advisable that you scan the trees periodically when rock hunting in bear country. You wouldn't want to find yourself in a fight with mama just because you stopped to pick up a rock under her nursery.

Bears are experts at keeping out of sight, unless they wish to be seen. They possess keen senses of smell and hearing. In the back country you greatly increase your odds of avoiding bears by making noise and walking with the wind at your back. This doesn't necessarily apply to front-country bears, which are not always afraid of people. They may find the smell of that tuna sandwich in your backpack intriguing enough to have a closer look.

If you happen to cross paths with a black bear here are a few things to remember:

- Don't let their clumsy appearance fool you. Bears can move very quickly.
- Drop anything you may be carrying that smells or looks like food and slowly back away.
- If a bear makes puffing, clicking, or grunting noises at you, stop what you are doing and get out of his way. DON'T RUN. Slowly back up then turn and walk away.
- Never make eye contact. Bears interpret this as a challenge.
- Unprovoked attacks on humans are rare and usually involve mothers with cubs or any bear with food.

Other Mammals

Other mammals found scattered across New Mexico include rabbits, raccoons, squirrels, deer, and coyotes. Of these, only the raccoon causes much in the way of trouble.

Because they are often carriers of rabies, raccoons are best avoided when possible. Daytime collectors will have no difficulty doing this, but overnight camping presents a challenge. Food should be stored in difficult-to-open containers. Really difficult. Raccoons have been known to open ice chests, fishing tackle boxes, and even trailer doors. The best practice is to remove all temptation by keeping foodstuffs locked inside a vehicle at night. (It is presumed you'll be doing this anyway because of the bears.)

Newcomers to the western states tend to feel a chill of fear the first time they hear the howl of a coyote. In some areas the coyotes are bolder than in others. You have little to fear, however, from these nighttime wanderers. They may sneak through your camp, but will do little damage other than waking you with their cry. Never approach coyotes or any other wildlife. If wild animals become a nuisance, you can usually frighten them away by making noise or throwing sticks and rocks.

Other Critters

New Mexico has two, somewhat undesirable, critters that rockhounds could come into contact with. One is the tarantula, the other is the scorpion. Both are limited to the dry desert areas of the state. Despite their reputations, bites from tarantulas and scorpions are rarely lethal, just painful. Tarantulas seem inclined to mind their own business and will simply run when disturbed. Scorpions are somewhat more difficult to avoid due to their pale tan coloring, which blends quite well with rocks and tent floors. Overnight campers would be well advised to carefully and thoroughly check their shoes before putting them on in the morning.

The intent of this discussion of potentially worrisome wildlife was not to discourage rockhounds from venturing into the New Mexico wilderness, but rather to better prepare them for any possibility. For more information contact the Forest Service office nearest your destination. They have detailed lists of wildlife that might be encountered. They can offer further advice on bear avoidance practices and will have current information on bears in specific localities.

ROCKHOUND RULES

Much of the land in New Mexico is owned by the government. That land is managed by several different agencies, each with distinctly different rules regarding rock collecting, and these rules are subject to change at anytime. Below is a list of the rules as they are currently interpreted. Collecting on reservation land is governed by individual tribes and is generally prohibited. Gathering of archeological resources, including, pottery, bones, arrowheads, and carvings, is prohibited on all public land.

Bureau of Land Management: Recreational collecting is allowed provided that all other rules are obeyed. These may include rules designed to preserve the land or protect the property or livestock of the land's current lessee or mineral claim owner. An example of this is at Tent Rocks (Site 12). Collecting is

It is tempting to break out the chisels to get at the Apache tears found in these tent rocks, but no climbing or defacing of the formations is allowed.

allowed, but climbing on the tent rocks is not. Additionally, collecting petrified wood is limited to 25 pounds plus one piece per person per day, with a yearly limit of 250 pounds.

U.S. Department of Agriculture Forest Service: Rock collecting in the national forests falls under the federal mining laws. Non-commercial hobby collecting is allowed, but collection of vertebrate fossils is prohibited. The 25-pound limit on petrified wood also applies. The "leave no trace" policy of the Forest Service should be strictly adhered to. Surface soil and vegetation cannot be removed without filing the paperwork to stake a mining claim. In cases where a Forest Service road crosses private property, no collecting is allowed until you reach the Forest Service property.

U.S. Department of Interior and National Park Service: No collecting is allowed on land within national parks, national monuments, national historic sites, or national conservation areas.

U.S. Department of Defense: No collecting is allowed on military installations.

New Mexico State Parks: No collecting is allowed in any state park.

New Mexico State Highway and Transportation Department: Highway right-of-ways under the management of this department are open to collecting when done for hobby purposes in a safe manner. Park well off the road, obey all warning signs, and cause no destruction to the property.

KIDS AND ROCKS

What is it with kids and rocks?! It's the question every mother must ask as she fishes them out of the bottom of the washing machine or finds them hidden in little piles under the bed. Rocks could be the best toy a kid will ever pick up. Here are the facts:

- They are generally free.
- They are in abundant supply.
- They come in an infinite range of colors, sizes, and shapes.
- Some of them sparkle and some change color when you get them wet.
- They don't wear out.
- They are educational.
- They don't talk, walk, wet, carry a sword, or require batteries.
- There are no Saturday morning cartoons about them.

In today's world where video games are fast replacing playgrounds, children are increasingly surrounded by technology. Yet a fascination with rocks is almost a universal thing with kids. With a bit of gentle guidance, a junior rockhound can quickly turn pocketfuls of treasure into a meaningful collection, learning a bit of geology, chemistry, and physics along the way. The process of mineral identification builds research and observation skills. It takes kids

Children need very little encouragement to begin a rock collection of their own.

outdoors, away from the computer and the TV screen, and puts them back in touch with nature.

The first lesson they need to learn is the difference between rocks and minerals. Simply put, minerals are the building blocks from which rocks are made. Lesson two should focus on the difference between the three rock groups: igneous, sedimentary, and metamorphic. Once they understand these basic principles, identifying their treasures gets a little easier.

Storing small collections is easily accomplished using clear plastic divided boxes, like those used to store fishing lures. Teach them the importance of including loose labels with each specimen. Color-coded labels help to increase awareness of rock groups, besides looking cool.

Encourage youngsters to expand their collections, but refrain from imposing your own ideals regarding color, size, quality, or quantity. Remember it's their collection. So what if they only like black rocks? Help them discover as many varieties of black rocks as possible.

When taking children into the field, it is important to choose sites that are appropriate to the age of the child. Accessibility is the key here. A four-hour drive followed by a 2-mile hike through the deserts of western New Mexico may be okay for a twelve-year-old experienced hiker, but probably not for a four-year-old. Sites should also be selected for their success ratio. There should be something to add to their collection from almost every site visited with children.

Teaching rockhounding safety and ethics is as important as teaching where to look for specific rocks. They should be taught the importance of safety goggles, good hiking boots, sunscreen, and drinking water.

Most importantly, as we share the satisfaction of this engaging hobby with the younger generation, we must teach them that it is sometimes better to leave more than we take. We should instill in them the idea that along with their passion for collecting the beauties of the earth, must also come the responsibility of preserving some it for future generations.

SITE 1 *WOOD AND AGATE NEAR CUBA*

Land type: Hills.
Elevation: 6,863 feet.
Best season: Spring, summer.
Land manager: Bureau of Land Management.
Material type: Display specimens and rocks for cutting and polishing.
Material: Petrified wood, agate, jasper.
Level of difficulty: Moderate.
Tools: Shovel.
Vehicle: Any.
Accommodations: Motels in Cuba; camping in Santa Fe National Forest.
Special attraction: Fishing on reservation lakes or in Santa Fe National Forest.
For more information: Fishing on Jemez Reservation at Holy Ghost Ponds or Dragonfly Ponds 505-834-7359.
Finding the site: Cuba is located on New Mexico Highway 44 north of Albuquerque. From Cuba, take NM 197 southwest approximately 5.5 miles to a dirt road heading north. Take that road approximately 2.3 miles before beginning your search.

Site 1 Wood and Agate Near Cuba & Site 2 Copper Minerals Near Cuba

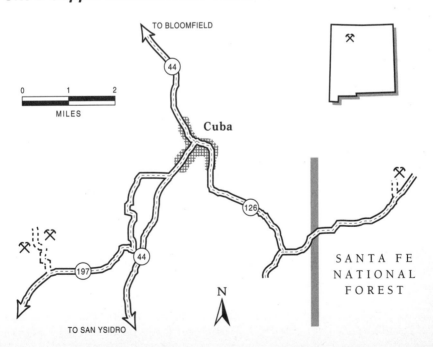

Rockhounding: The area west of Cuba may be the only place in the state where you can easily collect petrified wood large enough for your front flower bed. Very little of the wood found here is suitable for working, but there are specimen grade pieces in all sizes. Most of it is white and tan, and exhibits delightfully curved and twisted lineation.

The agate and jasper here is sparse, but of outstanding quality. Look for clear, brown, and black agate, occasionally bearing red inclusions. The jasper is caramel color, some pieces weighing up to 5 pounds.

Though much of the geology nearby is volcanic, Cuba perches at the edge of a large sedimentary basin. The mesas to the west are chiefly Jurassic and Cretaceous sandstone. Since these rocks are the source of the wood, larger concentrations abound closer to the mesas. The agate and jasper are the product of silica-laden water filling the cracks and crevices.

There are numerous dirt roads criss-crossing this deserted region. Further explorations could lead you to even better treasure. Take along a BLM map to avoid trespassing on private or reservation land, and don't forget to take plenty of water.

SITE 2 *COPPER MINERALS NEAR CUBA*

Land type: Mountains.
Elevation: 8,600 feet.
Best season: Summer.
Land manager: USDA Forest Service.
Material type: Mineral specimens and rocks for cutting and polishing.
Material: Malachite, chrysocolla.
Level of difficulty: Moderate.
Tools: Rock pick, shovel.
Vehicle: Any.
Accommodations: Motels in Cuba; camping in Santa Fe National Forest.
Special attractions: Fishing, scenic drives.
For more information: Santa Fe National Forest Cuba Ranger District 505-289-3265.
Finding the site: Cuba is located on New Mexico Highway 44 north of Albuquerque. From Cuba take NM 126 east about 8.9 miles to a private dirt road to the north. Cross the cattle guard and turn left at the second road. Continue approximately 0.5 mile until the road joins the former mine road up the mesa. Park here and hike the remainder of the way.

Rockhounding: You will know you're on the right road leading up to this old copper mine when you begin to see green. The road is littered with malachite and chrysocolla-bearing rock. The stuff on the road is so good in fact, you can leave here satisfied even if you don't make it to the top.

Why wouldn't you make it to the top, you ask? It is not because the hike is too strenuous, but simply that bears are particularly fond of this area. The

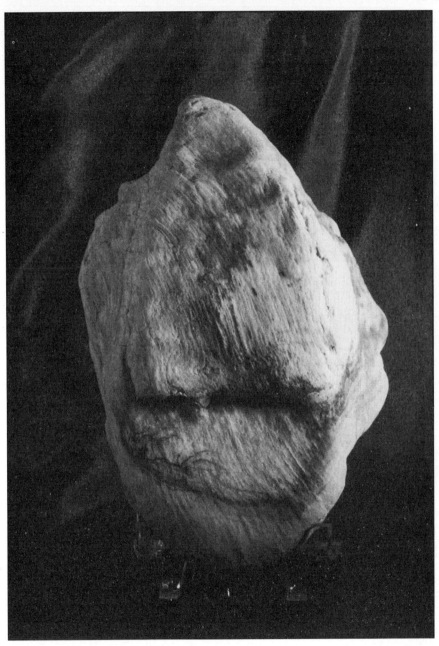

Specimen grade wood near Cuba is abundant.

mountainside overflows with wild berries. There is plenty of water nearby and not too many people.

At any rate, start up the road, eyes pealed to the ground and ears trained on the bushes. With luck and a bit of digging, you can easily take home a few workable malachite slivers. There are some nice chrysocolla specimens here as well.

After you find all the malachite you can haul, or have been chased away by the bears, try a scenic drive along NM 126. The road winds through the mountains and eventually ends up at Fenton Lake near Jemez Springs. There are rough camping areas along the way, or more civilized accommodations in and around Jemez Springs. Because dirt roads criss-cross the area, a Forest Service map is advisable.

SITE 3 *ALABASTER NEAR GALLINA*

Land type: Mountains.
Elevation: 7,362 feet.
Best season: Summer.
Land manager: USDA Forest Service.
Material type: Mineral specimens; rocks for carving.
Material: Alabaster.
Level of difficulty: Easy.
Tools: Rock pick, chisel.
Vehicle: Any.
Accommodations: Motels, RV parking in Cuba; camping in Santa Fe National Forest.
Special attractions: Camping, hiking.
For more information: Santa Fe National Forest Coyote Ranger District 505-638-5526.
Finding the site: Gallina is located northwest of Santa Fe, on New Mexico Highway 96 between Cuba and Coyote. From the west end of Gallina, turn south on Forest Service Road 76. The alabaster is found in the hills on the west side of the road, beginning about 0.65 miles from NM 96.

Rockhounding: Just outside Gallina, snow-white alabaster peaks tease you into believing that Santa Claus might really be hiding in New Mexico. Alabaster is the granular form of gypsum and has a hardness on the Mohs scale of only two. The material found here is carving grade, and you can choose your size. Small cobbles that have tumbled down from the cliff sides are scattered along the road. These carve with a pocket knife. For finer detail you could try Dremel tools.

Alabaster of this high quality is often in demand by artists. It is only recommended for work intended for indoor display, however. It tends to erode rather quickly if left to the elements. It may take some climbing and sweat-breaking work to get a sculpture-size piece. Be sure to take along hammers, gads, plenty of help, and water.

These gypsum beds are sandwiched between layers of Jurassic sedimentary rock. The mountains to the southeast are the northern rim of the Valles Caldera. Similar beds can be found in several areas surrounding the caldera and throughout the state, but these offer some of the finest grained material and are easily accessible.

SITE 4 *AGATE AND HEMATITE NEAR GALLINA*

Land type: Mountains.
Elevation: 7,760 feet.
Best season: Summer.
Land manager: USDA Forest Service.
Material type: Rocks for cutting and polishing.
Material: Agate, hematite.
Level of difficulty: Moderate to difficult.
Tools: None.
Vehicle: Any.
Accommodations: Motels and RV parking in Cuba; camping in Santa Fe National Forest.
Special attractions: Scenic drives.
For more information: Santa Fe National Forest Coyote Ranger District 505-638-5526.
Finding the site: Gallina is located northwest of Santa Fe on New Mexico Highway 96 between Cuba and Coyote. From the west end of Gallina, turn

Site 3 Alabaster Near Gallina &
Site 4 Agate and Hematite Near Gallina

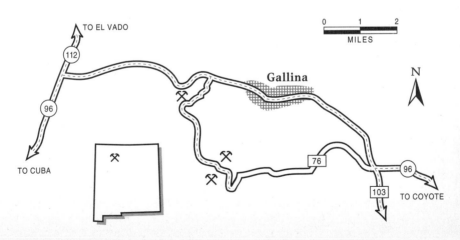

The agate found near Gallina is generally small with random color inclusions.

north on Forest Service Road 76. Look for dry washes and cobble beds beginning in about 3.5 miles.

Rockhounding: This area lies at the western edge of an abundant agate field that stretches along the northern rim of the Valles Caldera. The agate is mostly clear, brown, and black. Some pieces bear rusty red markings both inside and out. The sizes range from slivers and pebbles up to specimens weighing several pounds.

The hematite is much harder to find. It is in small, very smooth pieces, leading to the conclusion that it was washed into this valley from quite some distance. Because the stones present a smooth surface with which to begin, they should tumble very nicely. A few pieces large enough for cabbing are possible with some patience.

Forest Service Road 76 winds through a very scenic valley before returning to NM 96 east of Gallina. There are numerous logging roads branching off FR 76, but they are mostly dead-end. A Forest Service map is advisable before venturing off the main road.

SITE 5 *AGATE NEAR COYOTE*

Land type: Mountains.
Elevation: 7,662 feet.
Best season: Summer, fall.
Land manager: USDA Forest Service.
Material type: Rocks for cutting and polishing.
Material: Agate.
Level of difficulty: Easy.
Tools: None.
Vehicle: Any.
Accommodations: RV parking at Abiquiu Lake, camping in Santa Fe National Forest.
Special attraction: Fishing.
For more information: Santa Fe National Forest Coyote Ranger District 505-638-5526.

The bottle cap to the left of this large agate chunk puts the rock into scale.

Finding the site: Coyote is northwest of Española on New Mexico Highway 96. In Coyote mark mileage at Coyote Creek and travel 4.6 miles to Forest Service Road 172. Turn south. Travel 0.4 miles to FR 62. Turn left. Good collecting can be found along this road. Private property begins about 1 mile after turning onto FR 62.

Rockhounding: Boulders of agate litter the sides of this well-traveled road. Large- to medium-sized pieces are abundant throughout this region. Black, clear, white, and brown are the principal colors, but occasional pieces of orange or red hide here as well. Most of the inclusions are random swirls and splotches.

This is the center of the vast agate field stretching along the northern edge of the Valles Caldera. The agate most likely formed in cavities created in the native sandstone during the volatile volcanic period. As the softer matrix material eroded, the hard silica-based agate washed into low-lying areas.

The agate here takes a nice polish and often reveals interesting plays of color that are invisible in the rough. It is also possible to find pieces small enough for tumbling.

Try exploring other Forest Service roads in the region, but use a current Forest Service map to avoid trespassing on private property.

Site 5 Agate Near Coyote & Site 6 Agate Near Youngsville

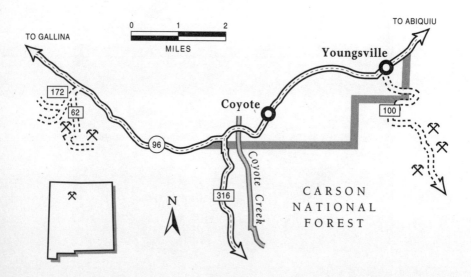

SITE 6 *AGATE NEAR YOUNGSVILLE*

Land type: Mountains.
Elevation: 7,200 feet.
Best season: Summer, fall.
Land manager: USDA Forest Service.
Material type: Rocks for cutting and polishing.
Material: Agate, jasper.
Level of difficulty: Easy.
Tools: None.
Vehicle: Any.
Accommodations: RV parking at Abiquiu Lake, camping in Santa Fe National Forest.
Special attraction: Fishing.
For more information: Santa Fe National Forest Coyote Ranger District 505-638-5526.
Finding the site: Youngsville is northwest of Española on New Mexico Highway 96. In Youngsville turn south on Forest Service Road 100. Travel about 3 miles before collecting, to make sure you are on federal land.

Rockhounding: This is the equivalent of one of those Easter egg hunts they hold in mall parking lots. There is no way to hide all the goodies. The object is just to gather up all you can stuff in your basket and sort it out when you get home. It is tempting to try to take home only the best pieces, but never trust dirty rocks seen in bright sunlight with naked eyes. They will fool you every time. Just remember that every piece holds potential beauty in the hands of the artisan.

The colors are black, white, clear, brown, and occasionally red. The pieces with a swirling combination of the principal colors are the prettiest. Most pieces are fist-sized or smaller, but don't rule out much larger pieces.

Take along plenty of water, a snake bite kit, and be sure to let somebody know where you plan to travel. This area is rather remote and the urge to dally is strong.

SITE 7 *AGATE NEAR ABIQUIU DAM*

Land type: Mountains.
Elevation: 6,514 feet.
Best season: Summer, fall.
Land manager: USDA Forest Service.
Material type: Rocks for cutting and polishing.
Material: Agate, jasper.
Level of difficulty: Easy.

Tools: None.
Vehicle: Any.
Accommodations: RV parking at Abiquiu Lake.
Special attractions: Fishing, Ruth Hall Museum of Paleontology at the Ghost Ranch.
For more information: Ghost Ranch 505-685-4312; Ruth Hall Museum 505-685-4333.
Finding the site: Abiquiu Dam is located northwest of Española near the junction of U.S. Highway 84 and New Mexico Highway 96. From US 84 turn west onto NM 96. Travel across the dam, safe pull-offs can be found at 2.25 and 2.8 miles from US 84. Search the hills overlooking the road.

Rockhounding: If you are traveling east to west along NM 96 the material found around Abiquiu Dam will whet your appetite. What lies ahead is the massive agate field that perches along the northern rim of the Valles Caldera. If you are traveling west to east, this will be your last chance to stop for one more rock.

The agate here, as throughout the field, is mostly black, brown, white, and clear. Watch for red splotches though. The pieces near the road tend to be small and picked over, but a short climb into the surrounding hills can often turn up larger specimens.

The fiery red hills that surround the reservoir are composed of Triassic beds, topped by Jurassic sandstone. Numerous dinosaur skeletons have been unearthed in the Triassic layers, including more than a thousand specimens of Coelophysis. It is one of the oldest known dinosaurs and is New Mexico's state fossil. The Ruth Hall Museum of Paleontology at Ghost Ranch has displays for viewing. Follow the signs north of the junction of NM 96 and US 84.

Site 7 Agate Near Abiquiu Dam

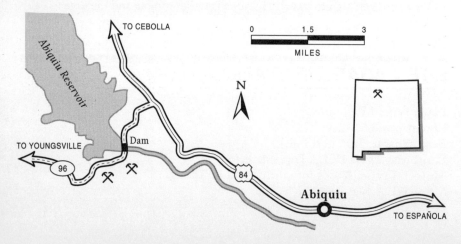

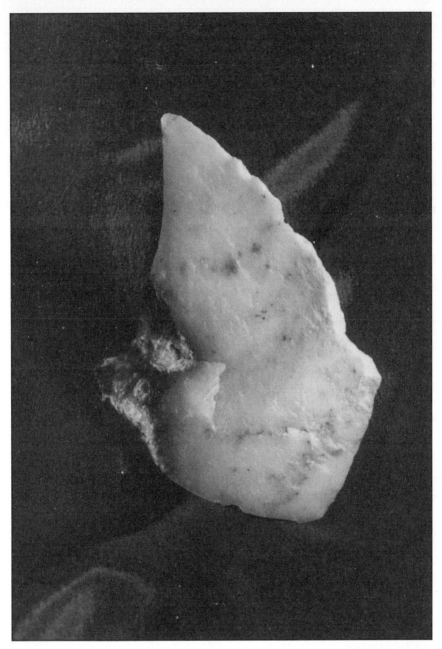

The agate found near Abiquiu Dam provides just a taste of the field that lies west of here.

SITE 8 *AGATE AND MINERALS NEAR LA MADERA*

Land type: Hills.
Elevation: 7,800 feet.
Best season: Summer, fall.
Land manager: USDA Forest Service.
Material type: Mineral specimens and rocks for cutting and polishing.
Material: Agate, chalcedony, jasper, calcite, quartz, calcite pseudomorphs after ilmenite.
Level of difficulty: Difficult.
Tools: Shovel.
Vehicle: Any.
Accommodations: Motels, RV parking in Española.
Special attractions: Ojo Caliente Mineral Springs.
For more information: Santa Fe National Forest Española Ranger District 505-753-7331; Ojo Caliente 505-583-2233.

Site 8 Agate and Minerals Near La Madera

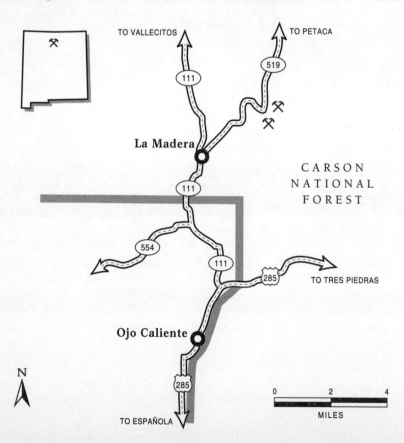

Finding the site: La Madera is located on New Mexico Highway 111 north of Española. Take U.S. Highway 285 north from Española. Just north of Ojo Caliente, turn northwest on NM 111. Approximately 5.1 miles after the turn, look for the junction with NM 519 on the right. Cross the bridge and continue approximately 2.2 miles. Immediately upon completing a sharp hairpin curve, find a safe place to pull off. The calcite is in the hills to the west of the road, and the chalcedony and agate are to the east.

Rockhounding: This is a site where you get back what you put into it. Rockhounds with patience and time will be rewarded with some very unusual calcite pseudomorphs and nice specimens of fluorescent chalcedony. There are also small pieces of clear agate and red jasper, but they also take some effort to find. Geodes reportedly litter the river bed as well.

Do not venture to this out-of-the-way location hoping to find good specimens in an hour or so. Ideally, plan for a half day here, perhaps in conjunction with a half day collecting on the Petaca Mine dumps.

SITE 9 *MINERALS ON THE PETACA MINE DUMPS*

Land type: Mountains.
Elevation: 8,400 feet.
Best season: Summer.
Land manager: USDA Forest Service.
Material type: Gemstones, mineral specimens.
Material: Muscovite, garnet, beryl, quartz, smoky quartz, amazonstone, ilmenite.
Level of difficulty: Moderate.
Tools: Hammer, rock pick.
Vehicle: Any.
Accommodations: Motels and RV parking in Española.
Special attraction: Rio Grande Gorge bridge.
For more information: Santa Fe National Forest Española Ranger District 505-753-7331.
Finding the site: Petaca is located in Rio Arriba County on New Mexico Highway 519 north of Española. Note: access from the south is not terribly difficult, but be aware that this is a tiny town with signs. Petaca is about 11 miles north of La Madera. Access from the north is more of a challenge. In Tres Piedras look for Forest Service Road 222, which intersects US Highway 285. The sign reads "to Las Tablas." Stay on this road to the Rio Tusas. The town just past the river is Petaca.

Once in Petaca, look for County Road 273. Follow it up the mountain to the dumps. The first dump is on the left side of the road about 1 mile from town.

Site 9 Minerals on the Petaca Mine Dumps

Rockhounding: Bring a lunch and plan to stay here at least half a day. Anything less and you will go home wondering what treasures you might have missed. The list of possible specimens from this mineral-rich area includes approximately fifty varieties, offering something for almost any hound.

The casual collector may be riveted by the near-perfect mica books. Veterans will enjoy sifting through the rubble for ilmenite, cassiterite, and uraninite. Gem collectors should look for the beryl, amazonite, smoky quartz, and garnets, all of which are relatively easy to find.

The beryl ranges from milky white to yellow green, and even some dark blue. At one time crystals of up to 8 feet long were reported in the area. Look for slivers and even some hexagonal crystals left in the dumps.

The garnet is abundant in the pegmatite. Most of the crystals are fractured and are wine to cinnamon colored. Careful examination of pegmatite fragments could produce a gem-quality stone.

The amazonite occurs chiefly as pearly fragments in the dumps. It is pale green, often with white or gray streaks. At one time, crystals with 12-foot diameters were taken from this district.

The ilmenite appears in tabular blocks. It is black and produces a semi-metallic streak. It is very slightly magnetic. The columbite and tantalite are black as well, but streak black and are not magnetic.

SITE 10 *OBSIDIAN NEAR PONDEROSA*

Land type: Mountains.
Elevation: 7,400 feet.
Best season: Summer.
Land manager: USDA Forest Service.
Material type: Rocks for cutting and polishing.
Material: Obsidian.
Level of difficulty: Moderate.
Tools: Shovel, rake.
Vehicle: Four-wheel-drive.
Accommodations: Bed and breakfasts, hotels, cabin rentals, and RV parking in Jemez Springs; camping in Santa Fe National Forest.

Site 10 Obsidian Near Ponderosa

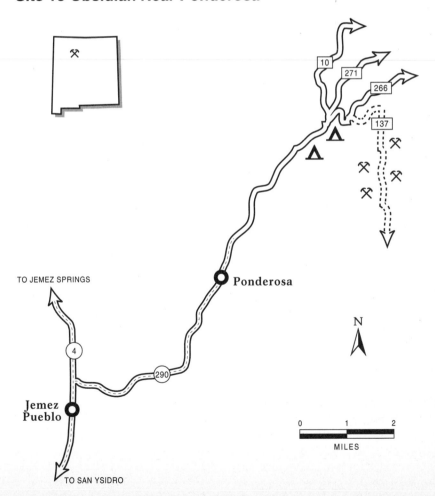

Special attractions: Scenic drives.

For more information: Santa Fe National Forest Jemez Ranger District 505-829-3535.

Finding the site: Ponderosa is located north of Albuquerque on New Mexico Highway 290, just off of the Jemez Indian Reservation. From NM 4 which runs through the pueblo of Jemez, turn east on NM 290. Pass through the town of Ponderosa, about 6 miles after turning. The pavement ends soon after passing through town. The road then becomes Forest Service Road 10. About 2.5 miles past Ponderosa, the road branches at the second Paliza Campground entrance. FR 10 turns off to the left, FR 271 is the center fork, and FR 266 is on the far right, passing the campground.

Take FR 266 to the right. About 1.65 miles after the campground, the road forks again. FR 266 continues straight. Take FR 137 to the right. The first sign of obsidian on the road is about 0.5 miles from the junction with FR 266.

Rockhounding: Exceptional nodules of opaque obsidian proliferate in this remote region. The road is listed as four-wheel-drive only on the Forest Service map, but can be handled (if dry) by most any utility vehicle. The easiest way to find the obsidian is to look on the road itself, walking with your back to the sun.

The pieces are a nice size for tumbling. Start them with a medium grit and work rather quickly through several stages of fine grit and polish. Dry plastic beads are ideal as a final finish.

The Paliza Campground offers a beautiful and secluded alternative to the campgrounds nearer Jemez Springs. There are four log shelters with fireplaces available, as well as numerous tent sites that can handle small trailers. Unfortunately there are no hookups, and the spaces are too small to accommodate large rigs.

If you are like most rockhounds, you can travel to stunningly beautiful sites and miss the scenery because habit has your eyes trained to the ground. This area of the Santa Fe National Forest is one worth lifting your head for, though. With a Forest Service map in hand, try venturing off onto the myriad of logging roads. Most are rough, but passable. You will find yourself transfixed by narrow corridors of pines, peaceful meadows, and heart-stopping vistas seen from knife-edge cliffs.

SITE 11 *OBSIDIAN NEAR JEMEZ SPRINGS*

Land type: Mountains.
Elevation: 8,150 feet.
Best season: Summer.
Land manager: USDA Forest Service.
Material type: Rocks for tumbling or display.
Material: Obsidian, snowflake obsidian.
Level of difficulty: Easy.

Tools: None.

Vehicle: Any.

Accommodations: Bed and breakfasts, hotels, cabin rentals, and RV parking in Jemez Springs. Camping in Santa Fe National Forest.

Special attractions: Fishing, sight-seeing, hot springs.

For more information: Santa Fe National Forest Jemez Ranger District 505-829-3535.

Finding the site: Jemez Springs is located on New Mexico Highway 4 north of Albuquerque. From Jemez Springs, continue along NM 4. At the community of La Cueva, the road forks. The left branch is NM 126 to Fenton Lake. Keep to the right to continue on NM 4. About 1.4 miles past the junction with NM 126, begin looking for obsidian-bearing road cuts.

Site 11 Obsidian Near Jemez Springs

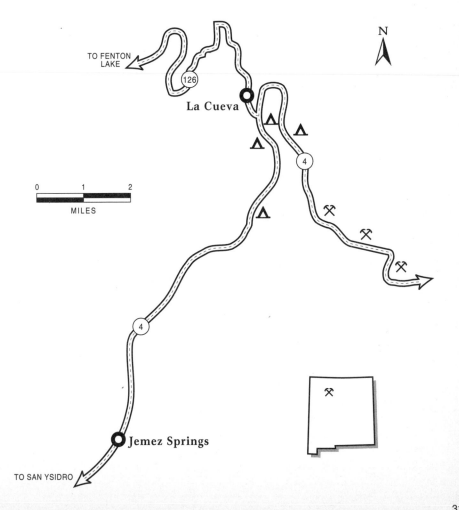

31

Rockhounding: At the New Mexico Museum of Natural History in Albuquerque they have a specimen of obsidian that probably weighs 50 pounds. If you have never been to Jemez Springs, that piece of rock seems unreal. But when you see the wall of obsidian found along NM 4, that piece in the museum begins to look like a sliver.

There are mountainsides of obsidian throughout the Jemez Valley. As you pass through the valley north of town, look up. Those shimmering cliffs to the right are solid obsidian. The road cut listed above is one of the few places where it's accessible, though.

The only problem with the material found at this site, however, is that because it contains bubbles and impurities, and has been exposed to temperature extremes, it fractures easily. Some of the small pieces tumble well. The good news is that there is plenty here, and you can haul away a big enough piece to impress your friends back home.

The Jemez Valley is known for its hot springs and mineral baths. The most famous are a little more than 3 miles north of Jemez Springs, just past Battleship Rock. There are two things you need to know before you decide to stop for a soak. First, it is a serious hike across the river and up the side of the mountain to reach the springs. Second, and most important, clothing is optional. An easier and perhaps more modest dip could be had at the bath house in town.

Snowflake obsidian nodules like this one are possible throughout the Jemez Valley.

SITE 12 *APACHE TEARS AT TENT ROCKS*

Land type: Hills.
Elevation: 5,737 feet.
Best season: Any.
Land manager: Bureau of Land Management.
Material type: Rocks for display.
Material: Obsidian, agate, volcanic bombs.
Level of difficulty: Moderate.
Tools: None.
Vehicle: Any.
Accommodations: Camping at Cochiti Lake; motels in Albuquerque or Santa Fe.
Special attractions: Bandelier National Monument, fishing, golf.
For more information: Tent Rocks information 505-761-8700; Bandelier National Monument 505-672-3861; Cochiti Lake Golf Course 505-465-2239.
Finding the Site: The tent rocks are located near Cochiti Pueblo between Santa Fe and Albuquerque. From Interstate Highway 25 take exit 259 onto New Mexico Highway 22 west. Travel 12.5 miles to Forest Service Road 268. Turn left. Travel approximately 1.7 miles to FR 266. Turn right. This dirt road crosses

Site 12 Apache Tears at Tent Rocks

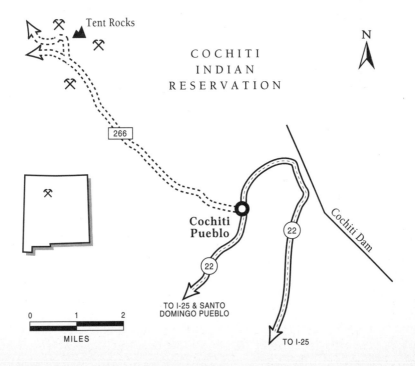

The ash-composed tent rocks sometimes erode into unusual shapes.

the Cochiti Reservation to the BLM land on which the tent rocks are located. Travel 3.2 miles to the BLM fence before beginning any collecting. Parking and hiking trails to the tent rocks are approximately 1.6 miles beyond the fence.

Rockhounding: This is one of the few sites in the state where obsidian occurs in the clear droplets known as Apache tears. They wash down from the unusual cone-shaped peaks of Bandelier Tuff that give this area its name.

Sadly though, rockhounds seem to have caught up with mother nature and keep the place picked clean of pieces larger than dime size. I visited the site as a child and found numerous specimens about the size of a quarter, but these are virtually impossible to find now. Therefore, I recommend picking up a few pieces and leaving the rest for the next person.

That leaves you free to search for the more unusual specimens found here. Watch for chunks of wavy white agate, some large enough to work. The best pieces seem to be nearest the peaks. The farther out you go, the more cherty the material gets.

Also look for volcanic bombs. They are round or oblong blobs of varying size. They take on their rounded shape as the result of being thrown through the air during a volcanic explosion. The exterior has a weathered but glassy appearance.

The formations known as "tent rocks" are scattered throughout the area surrounding the Valles Caldera. Some of them, like these near Cochiti, formed as the result of volcanic fumes rising through layers of ash. The ash surrounding the vent became harder. As the softer ash eroded, the hardened cone shape remained. In other areas, like in the Jemez Valley, the tents form as the result of erosion along vertical joints in the tuff.

SITE 13 *RIO PUERCO WOOD AND AGATE NEAR ALBUQUERQUE*

Land type: Rolling hills.
Elevation: 5,000 feet.
Best season: Any.
Land manager: Bureau of Land Management.
Material type: Rocks for cutting and polishing.
Material: Agate, jasper, petrified wood.
Level of difficulty: Moderate.
Tools: Shovel.
Vehicle: Any.
Accommodations: Motels and RV parking in Albuquerque.
Special attractions: New Mexico Museum of Natural History, Geology Museum at University of NM, shopping in Old Town.
For more information: New Mexico Museum of Natural History 505-841-8837; UNM Geology Museum 505-277-4204.
Finding the site: From Albuquerque take Interstate Highway 40 west to exit 140 at Rio Puerco. Immediately turn right onto the frontage road heading back to the east. At 4.4 miles turn north onto Lost Horizons Road. This road leads toward a former Air Force radar installation. At about 1.3 miles turn right onto a dirt road. Stay on the main road, avoiding any less-traveled branches. Good collecting begins at approximately 2.1 miles.

Rockhounding: This is the kind of site offering rewards for everyone, even those who don't care to do more than look along the side of the road. But beware, the more you look, the longer you may want to stay.

The jasper is brilliant red and gold. Most pieces are rather small. The most abundant find at this location is agate. Colors include clear, white, black, and brown. Most pieces exhibit only random swirls and splotches of color, but

Site 13 Rio Puerco Wood and Agate Near Albuquerque

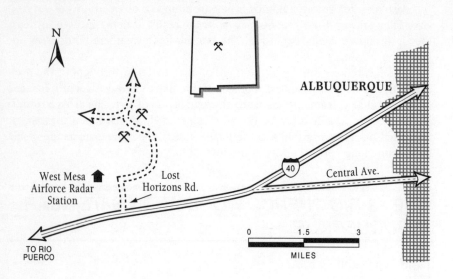

polishing sometimes reveals a more pronounced pattern. There are agates here of every size, many large enough for slabbing.

The petrified wood is not quite as plentiful, but the quality is outstanding in many cases. A careful eye may find dozens of small slivers, or even an occasional large piece up to 12 inches long.

Much of the land in this area is privately owned. Take care to avoid trespassing where posted. The BLM land is not continuous. As with most land managed by the BLM in New Mexico, this area is leased for grazing. Any holes you dig should be refilled to avoid injury to cattle.

The natural history museum in Albuquerque is a new-age museum. Rather than simply displaying cases of rocks, the museum presents the story of New Mexico through a series of hands-on exhibits and dioramas. The gem, mineral, and fossil displays, though not extensive, contain beautiful specimens.

After your tour of the museum, head down the street for some of New Mexico's best shopping in Old Town. The prices are not outrageous, and you can buy anything from books to jewelry to art.

SITE 14 *FOSSILS AND MINERALS OF THE SANDIA MOUNTAINS*

Land type: Mountains.
Elevation: 10,678 feet at Sandia Crest.
Best season: Summer.
Land manager: USDA Forest Service.
Material type: Fossils, mineral specimens.
Material: Fossils, hematite, orthoclase, malachite, barite, fluorite, chalcedony, tourmaline, gold.
Level of difficulty: Moderate to very difficult.
Tools: Hammer, rock pick, gold pan.
Vehicle: Any.
Accommodations: Rough camping in the national forest; motels and RV parking in Albuquerque.
Special attractions: Hiking, tramway ride.
For more information: Cibola National Forest Sandia Ranger District 505-281-3304.
Finding the site: The Sandia Mountains are located east of Albuquerque. There are two roads that lead to the top of Sandia Peak on the east side of the mountain. To take the northern route, take New Mexico Highway 165 east from Interstate Highway 25 in Bernalillo, toward Placitas. The pavement ends at 8.2 miles. Continue from there to where the road joins NM 536. Collecting can be done along the trail to the Sandia Man Cave, which is clearly marked at 3 miles after the pavement ends.

The southern route up the mountain is NM 536 from Tijeras. Excellent fossil collecting begins in the limestone roadcuts near the top.

Loose marine fossils are widespread near Sandia Crest.

Rockhounding: This is the type of place that could drive a rockhound crazy. There's some really good stuff here, but it's really hard to find. The exception is the abundant selection of brachiopods, bryozoans, and crinoid stems found in the sedimentary rock that caps Sandia Peak. The fossils are generally tightly encased in the matrix, but would lend themselves readily to an etching process.

If only the mineral specimens that have been reported here were as easy to find as the fossils. The list is quite long. It includes fluorite, barite, hematite, malachite, garnet, tourmaline, chalcedony, orthoclase, and of course, gold. For the best chance to find any minerals at all on the east side of the range, try sampling the stream beds that follow the northern route up the mountain.

Another possibility might be to hike the La Luz Trail that traverses the craggy west side, passing the La Luz Mine along the way. The easy way (easy is relative) is to take the Sandia Peak Tramway to the top, then hike down the 8-mile trail to the bottom. The western face of the mountain is mostly exposed and weathered Precambrian granite. It's a journey to remember even if you fail

Site 14 Fossils and Minerals of the Sandia Mountains

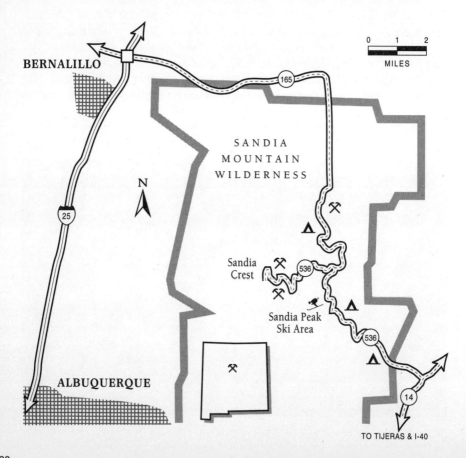

to find anything of value. The view will sneak up on you. When you least expect it, you find yourself looking over the tops of jagged rocks out across the Rio Grande Valley.

Be aware, though, that even experienced hikers have had to be rescued from these mountains. As simple as it might seem to just find the highest point and look down at the sprawling city of Albuquerque to find your way, people do get lost in the Sandias. Changes in the weather can surprise you, and deep canyons can disorient people. Stick to mapped trails if you decide to venture down either side of this beautiful giant.

SITE 15 *RIO PUERCO WOOD AND AGATE NEAR LOS LUNAS*

Land type: Rolling hills.
Elevation: 4,850 feet.
Best season: Any.
Land manager: New Mexico State Highway and Transportation Department.
Material type: Rocks for cutting and polishing.
Material: Wood, agate.
Level of difficulty: Easy.
Tools: None.
Vehicle: Any.
Accommodations: Motels and RV parking in Albuquerque.
Special attraction: Sightseeing in Albuquerque.
For more information: Albuquerque Convention and Visitors Bureau 800-284-2282.
Finding the site: From Interstate Highway 25 south of Albuquerque, take exit 203 to New Mexico Highway 6. This road crosses the Rio Puerco, but because the land on both sides is privately owned, collecting is limited to the roadsides. Good collecting is found approximately 10 miles from I-25 in the gravel beds exposed in the river breaks.

Rockhounding: The wood and agate found here are the same as that found in the area where the Rio Puerco passes west of Albuquerque. The wood is a varied mix. Some of it is well agatized and colorful, some is specimen quality only. The agate is mostly a combination of black, brown, and clear, with occasional finds of red.

This is serious snake country, so make lots of noise, carry a stick for prodding the bushes, and scan the ground before each footstep.

Site 15 Rio Puerco Wood and Agate Near Los Lunas

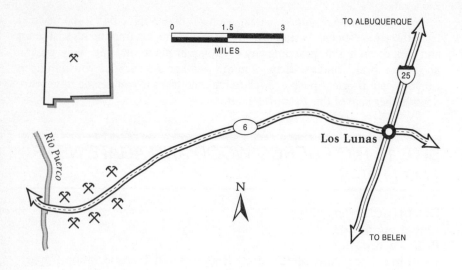

The wood found near the Rio Puerco is abundant and well agatized.

Opaque obsidian specimens litter the ground near Grants.

SITE 16 *OBSIDIAN NEAR GRANTS*

Land type: Mountains.
Elevation: 6,460 feet.
Best season: Summer, fall.
Land manager: USDA Forest Service.
Material type: Rocks for cutting and polishing.
Material: Obsidian nodules.
Level of difficulty: Easy.
Tools: None.
Vehicle: Any.
Accommodations: RV parking, motels in Grants; also trailer sites in Cibola National Forest.
Special attractions: New Mexico Mining Museum, Ice Cave.
For more information: Cibola National Forest Mount Taylor Ranger District 505-287-8833; New Mexico Mining Museum 1-800-748-2142; Ice Cave 505-783-4303.
Finding the site: Grants is located about 80 miles west of Albuquerque on Interstate Highway 40. From Grants, take New Mexico Highway 547 north toward Mount Taylor and the Cibola National Forest. Approximately 0.5 miles beyond mile marker 9, turn west on Forest Service Road 450. Travel about 2.5 miles to the collecting area. Prior to that, this road crosses private property, so collecting should be limited to the road itself.

Rockhounding: Some of the largest nodules of obsidian to be found in the state are scattered along this dirt road. The pieces are mostly opaque, with the average size matching a silver dollar (The real silver kind, not those S. B. Anthony things.) The best collecting is nearer the mountain; the quantities gradually lighten as you travel north into the flats.

The source of the volcanic glass in this region is most likely Mount Taylor. It has a history somewhat similar to that of Mount Saint Helens in Washington. Massive explosions sent debris, gas, and ash hurtling into the air. These explosions alternated with steaming mud flows. The most recent eruption took place about 2 million years ago.

The much younger Malpais lava beds near Grants however, flowed from smaller craters to the south. These erupted as recently as one thousand years ago. For a closer look at the Malpais, travel south on NM 53 to the Ice Caves. The caves are really lava tubes. The ice in the tubes forms as rain seeps through the lava. Because the lava acts as a prime insulator, the ice never melts. It measures 20 feet deep, with the deepest ice dating to the year A.D. 170. The trip to the Ice Cave also affords an ideal lookout point into the nearby craters.

SITE 17 *GARNET AND TOPAZ NEAR GRANTS*

Land type: Mountains.
Elevation: 6,460 feet.
Best season: Summer, fall.
Land manager: USDA Forest Service.
Material type: Gemstones, rocks for cutting and polishing.
Material: Garnet, topaz, obsidian.
Level of difficulty: Difficult.
Tools: Hammer, rock pick.
Vehicle: Any.
Accommodations: RV parking, motels in Grants; trailer sites in Cibola National Forest.
Special attractions: New Mexico Mining Museum, Chaco Culture National Historical Site.
For more information: Cibola National Forest Mount Taylor Ranger District 505-287-8833; New Mexico Mining Museum 1-800-748-2142; Chaco Canyon 505-988-6716.
Finding the Site: In Grants take New Mexico Highway 547 north towards Mount Taylor and the Cibola National Forest. Near milepost 8 look for an area where the road cuts through the hillside, exposing the clay-colored tuff.

Rockhounding: Small topaz and garnet crystals are found in the rhyolite leading up to Mount Taylor. Some loose specimens may be found by sifting through the crumbles, but the best means of finding them is by breaking open suspected chunks of rock.

Rhyolite is a light-weight, light-colored porous rock, formed at or near the top of a lava flow. It often contains crystals, as it does in this area. Garnet and topaz commonly form in rhyolites and other igneous rock, and in rock of metamorphic origin. Also look for small obsidian pebbles in these same hills.

Site 16 Obsidian Near Grants &
Site 17 Garnet and Topaz Near Grants &
Site 18 Selenite Near Grants &
Site 19 Carnotite Near Grants

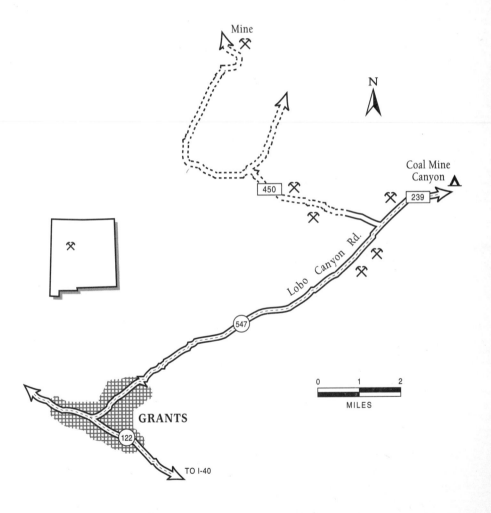

SITE 18 *SELENITE NEAR GRANTS*

Land type: Mountains.
Elevation: 6,460 feet.
Best season: Summer.
Land manager: USDA Forest Service.
Material type: Mineral specimens.
Material: Selenite.
Level of difficulty: Easy.
Tools: None.
Vehicle: Any.
Accommodations: RV parking, motels in Grants; trailer sites in Cibola National Forest.
Special attractions: New Mexico Mining Museum, Chaco Culture National Historical Site.
For more information: Cibola National Forest Mount Taylor Ranger District 505-287-8833; New Mexico Mining Museum 1-800-748-2142; Chaco Canyon 505-988-6716.
Finding the Site: Grants is located about 80 miles west of Albuquerque on Interstate Highway 40. From Grants, take New Mexico Highway 547 north toward Mount Taylor and the Cibola National Forest. Begin searching road cuts for evidence of the selenite in road cuts just past mile post 8.

Rockhounding: In areas where the older Triassic and Jurassic rocks are exposed in this volatile volcanic region, there are quite frequently gypsum deposits. As you pass through Lobo Canyon heading up the side of Mount Taylor, look for the white outcroppings, including a now-abandoned mining operation. At the base of the cliffs look for gypsum in its crystalline form: selenite.

The selenite found here is generally in tabular crystals. Large sheets of the selenite from this area were once used for window panes. Careful searching can often produce more uncommon specimens though, including scepters and crosses. Both are very fragile and will only be found by gentle digging in the soft clay.

SITE 19 *CARNOTITE NEAR GRANTS*

Land type: Mountains.
Elevation: 6,460 feet.
Best season: Summer.
Land manager: Bureau of Land Management.
Material type: Mineral specimens.
Material: Carnotite.
Level of difficulty: Moderate.

Tools: None.

Vehicle: Utility.

Accommodations: RV parking, motels in Grants; also trailer sites in Cibola National Forest.

Special attraction: New Mexico Mining Museum.

For more information: Cibola National Forest Mount Taylor Ranger District 505-287-8833; New Mexico Mining Museum 1-800-748-2142.

Finding the site: Grants is located about 80 miles west of Albuquerque on Interstate Highway 40. From Grants, take New Mexico Highway 547 north toward Mount Taylor and the Cibola National Forest. Approximately 0.5 miles beyond mile marker 9, turn west on Forest Service Road 450. Travel about 5.9 miles to the first set of mine dumps.

Rockhounding: Carnotite is a secondary uranium ore, and as such is radioactive. That said, this sight offers serious mineral hounds an opportunity to add small specimens of the brilliant yellow carnotite to their collections. The specimens found here are coarse and granular, and are most easily found in combination with other rock.

The history of Grants is founded upon the heavy uranium mining that took place here until the last decade. A visit to the New Mexico Mining Museum in town provides insight into the industry. The museum is small, but packed with information. There are mineral displays, outstanding video presentations, and even a trip into the depths of a mine mock-up that allows close inspection of the equipment and techniques used.

SITE 20 *BLUEWATER WOOD*

Land type: Hills.

Elevation: 6,400 feet.

Best season: Any.

Land manager: Various.

Material type: Display specimens.

Material: Petrified wood.

Level of difficulty: Difficult.

Tools: None.

Vehicle: Any.

Accommodations: Motels and RV parking in Grants; camping at Bluewater Lake State Park or in Cibola National Forest.

Special attraction: Fishing.

For more information: Cibola National Forest Mount Taylor Ranger District 505-287-8833; Bluewater State Park 505-876-2391; Navajo Indian Reservation 602-871-6659.

Finding the site: Bluewater Lake State Park is located south of Interstate Highway 40 between Grants and Gallup. From I-40, exit to New Mexico

Site 20 Bluewater Wood

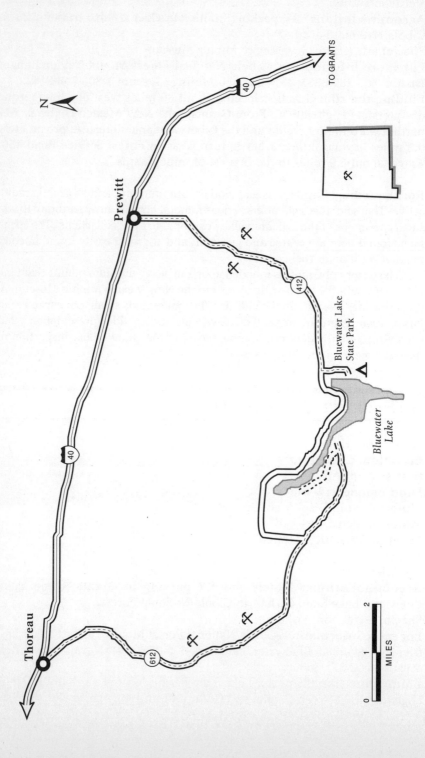

Highway 412 near Prewitt. Travel south on this road to the state park, stopping to check rocky roadsides along the way. Two other roads to check are NM 612 south from Thoreau and NM 400 south to Fort Wingate. Both roads lead into the Cibola National Forest where collecting is possible.

Rockhounding: Some of the wood from this region between Grants and Gallup has been identified as *Araucarioxylon arizonicum*, the same species of conifer found in Arizona's petrified forest. Be aware that specimens are rather difficult to find, often due to heavy vegetation. Check all rocky areas, including washes and stream beds. This wood is worth looking for.

Not all specimens are well agatized, but those that are exhibit outstanding color, from deep red to black. Sizes range from small pebbles to chunks weighing in at several pounds. Presumably the largest specimen unearthed here was a log measuring 11 feet long and more than 2 feet in diameter.

A great deal of wood has also been reportedly found in northern McKinley County, but that land is part of the Navajo Reservation. No collecting is allowed without permission, which may or may not be granted.

SITE 21 *HARDING PEGMATITE MINE NEAR DIXON*

Land type: Mountains.
Elevation: 7,000 feet.
Best season: Spring, summer.
Land manager: University of New Mexico.
Material type: Gemstones, mineral specimens.
Material: Lepidolite, beryl, rose muscovite, quartz, microcline, spodumene, tantalite-columbite, optical grade calcite.
Level of difficulty: Moderate.
Tools: Hammer, rock pick.
Vehicle: Any.
Accommodations: Motels and RV parks within 25 miles (Taos or Española).
Special attractions: Rio Grande river rafting.
For more information: University of NM Department of Earth and Planetary Sciences 505-277-4204.
Finding the site: Dixon is located on New Mexico Highway 75, just off of NM 68 between Taos and Española. In Dixon stay on NM 75 about 1.5 miles to Rio Arriba County Road 63. Turn right. Follow the road to house number 72 on the right. This is the home of the mine caretaker, Gilbert Griego. You must stop here to sign a release and get directions to the mine. If no one is home, try the homes of Alice Griego, number 36, or Bernabe Griego, number 71.

Rockhounding: The Harding Pegmatite Mine offers mineral collectors a unique opportunity to gather outstanding examples of several minerals. The beautiful purple lepidolite is the easiest to collect, because it is everywhere. It is difficult to distinguish from the rose muscovite, however. Look for the

Site 21 Harding Pegmatite Mine Near Dixon

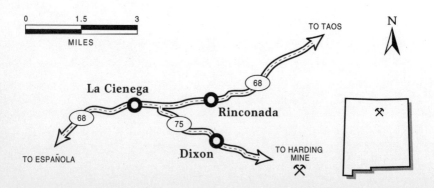

It is permissible to step into the openings of the tunnels at the Harding Pegmatite Mine.

slightly bluish tint in the lepidolite. Careful sifting through the dumps can produce a wide array of other finds.

The mine has produced numerous museum-quality specimens of spodumene, some more than 10 feet long. Because the crystals are prone to fracturing, look for slivers left behind in the dumps. They are generally greenish in color, but may be pink as well. The calcite is found by following the upper trail beyond the main quarry to the Iceberg Pit.

Prospectors first came to the Harding district seeking gold in the quartz outcrops. The mine began shipping the lithium ore lepidolite in 1919. Mining of beryl began in the 1940s and continued through the 1950s. The mine now belongs to the University of New Mexico, which uses it for research and education purposes.

SITE 22 *GARNET AND STAUROLITE CROSSES NEAR TAOS*

Land type: Mountains.
Elevation: 6,900 feet.
Best season: Summer.
Land manager: USDA Forest Service.
Material type: Gemstone, mineral specimens.
Material: Garnet, staurolite.
Level of difficulty: Very difficult.
Tools: Hammer, rock pick.
Vehicle: Four-wheel-drive with short wheel base.
Accommodations: Motels and RV parking in Taos.
Special attractions: Shopping, sightseeing in Taos.
For more information: Carson National Forest Camino Real Ranger District Penasco, 505-587-2255.
Finding the site: From Taos take New Mexico Highway 68 south. Because the road leading to the site is difficult to find, mark mileage at the intersection of NM 585 and NM 68. At 10.3 miles look for the dirt road leading into the hills. From Pilar take NM 68 north to mile marker 33. The dirt road is just past this marker. At 0.2 miles up the road a large boulder blocks the way. Some four-wheel-drives can get around it and make it most of the way up the 2-mile road to the collecting area. Use caution when assessing road conditions. Mud can be deceptively deep after spring thaw. This site presents a nice place to hike.

Rockhounding: It seems that every rockhound that has ever set foot in New Mexico has tried their luck at finding the prized staurolite crosses near Taos. Some collectors have gone home with smiles on their faces; many have not. Perhaps it is their very elusiveness that keeps people coming. I spoke to one collector that had been here year after year, claiming only five good crosses

Site 22 Garnet and Staurolite Crosses Near Taos

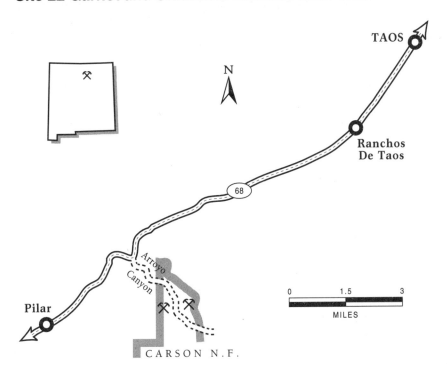

Not all 4x4's can navigate the road to the fairy crosses near Taos.

with a cost of several hundred hours of hiking and rock splitting. But she was smiling when she described those five crosses.

For those who have not tried it, here's the drill. Staurolite is an iron and aluminum silicate. The color is gray to black. It forms crystals twinned at between 60 and 90 degrees. They are usually no more than 1 inch across and are embedded in the mica schist along the road. The only practical way to find the crosses is to split pieces of the schist. Do not overlook the plum colored garnets in your quest for the crosses.

This is a good place to test out your bear avoidance practices. The area is remote, and the wild berries are plentiful. Watch for signs of recent activity and make lots of noise.

SITE 23 *MOLYBDENUM MINES NEAR QUESTA*

Land type: Mountains.
Elevation: 8,700 feet.
Best season: Summer.
Land manager: USDA Forest Service.
Material type: Mineral Specimens.
Material: Molybdenite, selenite.
Level of difficulty: Moderate to difficult.
Tools: None.
Vehicle: Any.
Accommodations: Motels and RV parking in Red River; camping in Carson National Forest.
Special attractions: Camping and hiking.
For more information: Carson National Forest Questa Ranger District 505-586-0520.
Finding the site: The Questa Molybdenum Mines are located on New Mexico Highway 38 between Red River and Questa. From Red River travel west on NM 38. Look for the dumps and prospect pits on the north side of the road about 2 miles west of town.

Rockhounding: This is an on-the-way site. If you happen to be passing through Red River or Questa, stop for a quick look around. The molybdenite is difficult to find, but micro-mounters may find a few specimens worth the trouble. Look for the blue gray metallic mineral associated with quartz. The selenite occurs in nice tabular crystals throughout the prospect pits and dumps.

Across the road the Red River makes a nice spot to scour the river rocks for treasure brought in from afar. Occasional finds include well-weathered black agate and petrified wood.

Site 23 Molybdenum Mines Near Questa & Site 24 Orthoclase Crystals Near Red

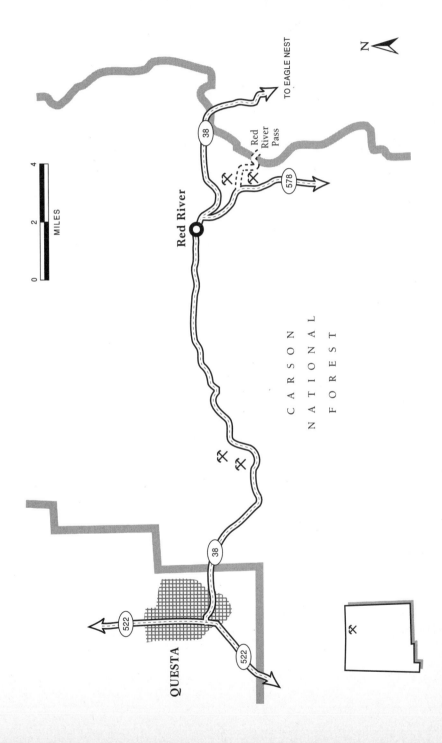

SITE 24 *ORTHOCLASE CRYSTALS NEAR RED RIVER*

Land type: Mountains.
Elevation: 8,750 feet.
Best season: Summer.
Land manager: USDA Forest Service.
Material type: Mineral specimens.
Material: Orthoclase crystals in matrix.
Level of difficulty: Difficult.
Tools: Chisels, gads, hammer.
Vehicle: Utility.
Accommodations: Motels and RV parking in Red River.
Special attractions: Shopping in Red River; summer chair lift rides in Red River.
For more information: Carson National Forest Questa Ranger District 505-586-0520; chair lift rides 505-754-2382.
Finding the Site: From Red River travel southeast on New Mexico Highway 578 for about 1.9 miles. Look for the old Red River Pass Road on the left. The road is marked four-wheel-drive only, but the rock bearing the crystals is only 0.3 miles up the road. Any utility vehicle should have no difficulty. Look for the crystal-bearing, granite-like rock in the center of the first main switchback.

Rockhounding: There are several localities throughout New Mexico where quality orthoclase crystals can be collected, but this site near Red River is probably the most accessible. Heavily weathered crystals are easily located in the broken fragments of rock, but fresh crystals can be exposed with some splitting.

It is advisable to simply load up as many chunks as you can haul and move on. There are two reasons. The first is that exposing good crystal specimens is a painstaking process, with better results often achieved in a less hurried situation. The second is the lack of off-road parking on this narrow dirt road.

The crystals here occur in what is called a porphyry. Porphyritic rock is a fine-grained igneous rock in which larger crystals are encased. This porphyry is a monzonite, one of several rocks commonly called granite. What this means to the collector is a hardness that increases the level of difficulty in exposing the crystals.

Hammers can be used to break away the initial pieces of rock, until the edges of a crystal become exposed. The remaining matrix will need to be carefully chipped away with delicate picks to avoid marring the orthoclase. Power hand tools may be useful in this process.

SITE 25 *ROSE MUSCOVITE NEAR EAGLE NEST*

Land type: Mountains.
Elevation: 8,700 feet.
Best season: Summer.
Land manager: New Mexico State Highway Department.
Material type: Mineral specimens.
Material: Rose muscovite.
Level of difficulty: Easy.
Tools: Pick.
Vehicle: Any.
Accommodations: Motels, RV parking, cabin rentals in Eagle Nest or Red River; camping in Carson National Forest.
Special attractions: Elizabethtown ghost town, fishing.
For more information: Carson National Forest Questa Ranger District 505-586-0520.

Site 25 Rose Muscovite Near Eagle Nest & Site 26 Graphic Granite in Cimarron Canyon

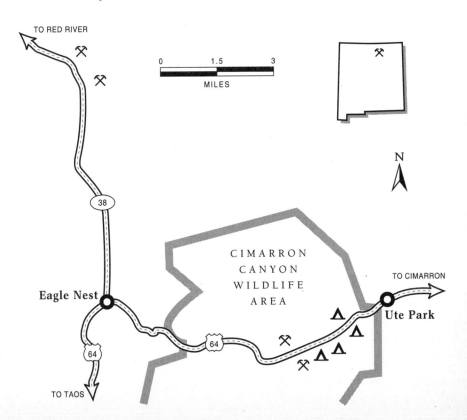

The rose muscovite in this road cut shimmers purple in the morning light.

Finding the site: Eagle Nest is located at the junction of U.S. Highway 64 and New Mexico Highway 38, on the eastern edge of the "enchanted circle" that connects Taos and Red River. In Eagle Nest turn north on NM 38. Travel 8.1 miles to the muscovite-bearing road cut.

Rockhounding: If you have traveled NM 38 from Eagle Nest to Red River but never noticed this purple mountain, don't feel bad. It could have been the wrong time of day. But early in the morning, as the sun peaks over the mountains, this entire road cut screams out in vivid purple. It takes a good pair of sun glasses to cut the tin-foil glare.

The muscovite bears a striking resemblance to the lepidolite found elsewhere in Taos County and is often mistaken for the other purple mineral by some collectors. Though the two minerals are sometimes found in association, no lepidolite has ever been recorded from this site.

About 5 miles north of Eagle Nest stands a solitary building just off the highway. This is all that remains of one of the largest and most famous New Mexico gold mining towns. The boom in Elizabethtown started in 1867, and the population quickly soared to over 7,000. There is a legend in these parts about a lost load of gold, that supposedly was buried in a flood. Short of finding the lost gold, a few hours spent panning the local creeks could prove moderately prosperous.

SITE 26 *GRAPHIC GRANITE IN CIMARRON CANYON*

Land type: Mountains.
Elevation: 7,700 feet.
Best season: Summer.
Land manager: USDA Forest Service.
Material type: Rocks for cutting and polishing.
Material: Granite.
Level of difficulty: Moderate.
Tools: None.
Vehicle: Any.
Accommodations: Motels in either Cimarron or Eagle Nest; camping at Cimarron Canyon State Park.
Special attractions: Fishing, hiking.
For more information: Cimarron Canyon State Park 505-377-6271.
Finding the site: Cimarron Canyon is located along U.S. Highway 64 between Raton and Taos. The best site for collecting the granite is in a road cut located 4.2 miles west of the Maverick Campground and 10.5 miles east of the junction with New Mexico Highway 38 in Eagle Nest.

Rockhounding: Little squiggly lines that look as though a three- year-old colored these rocks with a crayon create some of the best examples of graphic granite found in the state. Pieces ranging in size from 1 to 15 pounds are not terribly difficult to find. Large quartz crystals, set against a peach-colored blend of mica and feldspar, make up the graphic pattern.

The massive crystal structures found in pegmatic granite blocks such as these are the result of rapid crystallization of minerals present in magma. Finer-grained granite results from a much slower cooling process.

The geology of Cimarron Canyon is quite varied. The rock at the east end of the canyon near Ute Park is Pierre Shale. It is this gray, crumbly material that causes numerous landslides in the initial road cuts leading into the canyon. North of the canyon stands Baldy Peak, home of the famous Aztec Gold Mine. The mine lies in a glacier-cut valley near the timberline. Unfortunately for rockhounds, most of the mountain including the mine, belongs to the Philmont Boy Scout Ranch. Access to it would involve volunteering to go on a wilderness trek several days long with a Scout troop.

Another interesting feature in the canyon is known as the Palisades. These jagged rock teeth were cut by vertical cooling joints of igneous rock protruding through horizontal rock layers. Look for the Palisades on the north side of the road. Just west of the Palisades, look for dark gray glittery rock known as gabbro. It forms from very fluid magma found near the Earth's mantle.

SITE 27 *FOSSILS NEAR RATON*

Land type: Mountains.
Elevation: 6,000 feet.
Best season: Summer, fall.
Land manager: New Mexico State Highway and Transportation Department.
Material type: Fossils in matrix.
Material: Fossils.
Level of difficulty: Difficult.
Tools: Pick.
Vehicle: Any.
Accommodations: Motels and RV parking in Raton.
Special attractions: Horse racing; Capulin Volcano National Monument.
For more information: Capulin National Monument 505-278-2201.
Finding the Site: Raton is located on Interstate Highway 25 near the Colorado border. From Raton take U.S. Highway 64/87 east. About 16 miles from the junction with I-25, look for fossil-bearing shale road cuts.

Rockhounding: As the last sea to invade New Mexico departed, it left behind the soft shale and sandstone layers that form the walls of these mesas outside Raton. The fossils encased here are the remains of Upper Cretaceous and Lower Tertiary marine mollusks. Most specimens are small, about the size of a dime. Larger examples can be found, though, with some persistence.

Site 27 Fossils Near Raton

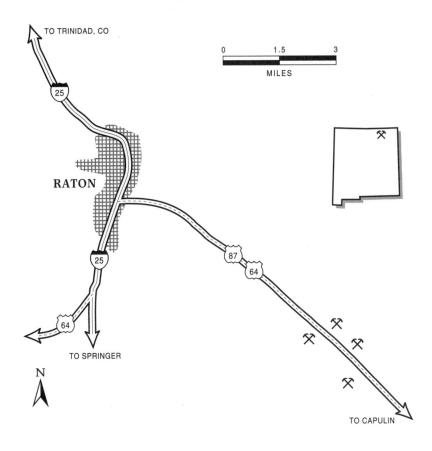

To get at the fossils it is necessary to carefully split the layers of shale. Stop at several road cuts, sampling the shale as you go. Some areas will be more productive than others. In general, though, the darker shales seem to bear the most fossils.

Do not overlook specimens that have eroded out of the matrix. Careful examination of the loose scrabble in some of the road cuts can produce a nice piece or two.

SITE 28 *MINERALS AT THE TERRERO MINE*

Land type: Mountains.
Elevation: 7,880 feet.
Best season: Summer.
Land manager: USDA Forest Service.
Material type: Mineral specimens, rocks for cutting and polishing.
Material: Pyrite, chalcopyrite, galena, barite, fluorite, agate.
Level of difficulty: Moderate.
Tools: Shovel, water.
Vehicle: Any.
Accommodations: Motel in Pecos, camping in Santa Fe National Forest.
Special attractions: Pecos National Historical Park.
For more information: Santa Fe National Forest Pecos/Las Vegas Ranger District 505-757-6121; Pecos National Historical Park 505-757-6032.
Finding the site: The Terrero Mine dumps are located on New Mexico Highway 63, north of Pecos. From Pecos take NM 63 north for about 13.4 miles to the Terrero Store. The mine dumps are adjacent to the road about 1 mile farther.

Rockhounding: The majority of the dumps here at Terrero have been fenced off and are no longer accessible for collecting due to "hazardous" levels of lead. Until a clean-up effort takes place, however, there are areas where dumps have overflowed through the fences and even across the road. These places afford the collector one last chance to sample the tiny treasures found here before they disappear.

Look for micro-mount specimens of pyrite, chalcopyrite, galena, and fluorite. The barite is plentiful, many examples forming interesting collections of saw-tooth crystals.

If you get to Terrero and find it all swept away, or if minerals are not your thing, take heart. Check the road cuts all along this beautiful valley that is the gateway into the heart of the Sangre de Cristo Mountains. There are some very nice layers of agate found in the country rock. The principal color is a milky gray, but most pieces are shot through with bright red bands.

Look for broken pieces scattered in the road cuts. The agate usually appears as thin bands, but some layers are up to 2 inches thick. A few pieces contain quartz-lined vugs as well. Dark mud coats most of these rocks, so it may take some washing to find the good stuff.

The red most likely resulted from the addition of iron oxides to the silica mixture, as the agate formed in pockets of the sand and siltstone. The same vivid reds are visible in the hillsides in various spots in this valley and to the west.

Site 28 Minerals at the Terrero Mine

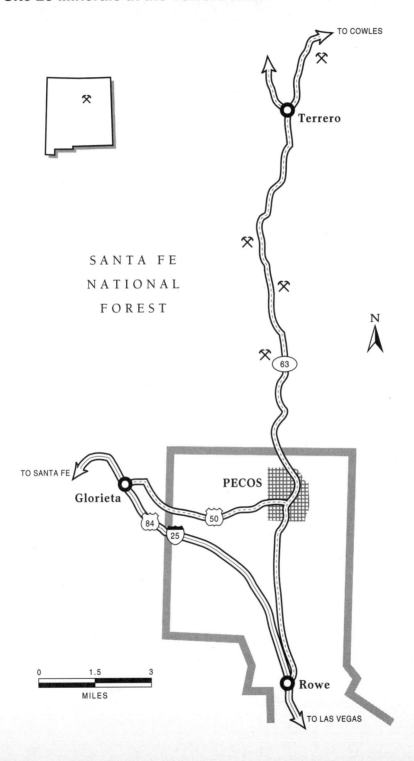

SITE 29 *JASPER AND WOOD NEAR GALISTEO*

Land type: Hills.
Elevation: 5,496 feet.
Best season: Summer.
Land manager: New Mexico State Highway and Transportation Department.
Material type: Rocks for tumbling.
Material: Petrified wood, jasper.
Level of difficulty: Easy.
Tools: None.
Vehicle: Any.
Accommodations: Motels and RV parking in Santa Fe.
Special attraction: Turquoise Trail.
For more information: A complete guide to the Turquoise Trail is published by the Turquoise Trail Association, Box 693, Albuquerque, NM 87103.

Site 29 Jasper and Wood Near Galisteo

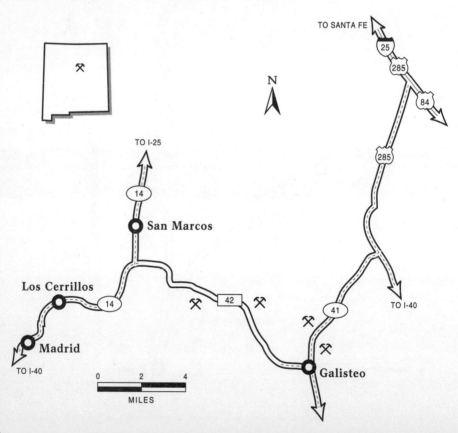

Finding the site: Galisteo is located on New Mexico Highway 41 south of Santa Fe. From Interstate Highway 25 south of Santa Fe, exit to U.S. Highway 285. Travel 6.8 miles to the junction with NM 41. Turn right. Begin searching any rocky road cut after turning onto NM 41. In Galisteo turn west on County Road 42. This road leads to NM 14 near Cerrillos, which is part of the Turquoise Trail.

Rockhounding: The wood found around Galisteo has historically been some of the finest in the state. The problem now is that most of it is on private property. The area has been subdivided and a housing boom is currently taking place just west of the town, making it somewhat of a suburb of Santa Fe.

What this means to collectors is that the wood is generally only available in road cuts or road gradings. Most collectors will leave here with only a handful of well agatized slivers.

The jasper is not terribly plentiful, but a few small pieces suitable for tumbling can be found in almost any road cut. Most of the material is red, but there are some green pieces as well. Look also for pieces of banded gray flint.

Many collectors come to this area hoping to search for turquoise in addition to the jasper and wood. The best place to look for that is in the rock shops in Los Cerrillos. The mines are all privately owned, with no collecting allowed at the time of this writing. Large specimens of the wood can also be purchased here.

The historical mining town of Los Cerrillos once was large enough to support twenty-one saloons and four hotels. Today the town is a quiet hamlet tucked away amid tall cottonwoods. It is this sleepy, lost city look that has made it an ideal setting for filming western movies in recent years.

SITE 30 *FOSSILS AT STORRIE LAKE*

Land type: Hills.
Elevation: 6,400 feet.
Best season: Summer, fall.
Land manager: New Mexico State Highway and Transportation Department.
Material type: Fossils in matrix.
Material: Fossils.
Level of difficulty: Easy.
Tools: None.
Vehicle: Any.
Accommodations: Camping at Storrie Lake State Park; RV parking and motels in Las Vegas.
Special attractions: Fishing, Montezuma Castle on the grounds of the Armand Hammer United World College of the Americas.
For more information: Storrie Lake 505-425-7278; Montezuma Castle 505-454-4277.

Finding the site: Storrie Lake is located north of Las Vegas on New Mexico Highway 518. From Las Vegas take NM 518 (7th Street) north about 4 miles. After crossing the dam, look for fossil-bearing road cuts along the west side of the road.

Rockhounding: Tiny Cretaceous gastropods and cephalopods seem ready to slither off the rock in your hand. These specimens near Las Vegas are so well preserved that they appear to need nothing but a bit of warm salt water to bring them back to life.

The shale at this site is broken and very crumbly. Almost any piece you pick up contains fossils. All it takes is a bit of cleaning to reveal excellent specimens. Further enhancements, such as etching, can expose even more of the delicate shells.

The shale exposed here is part of a readily identifiable formation deposited here by the last of the inland seas. Pierre Shale stretches from here northward to South Dakota. Fossil-bearing outcrops can be found throughout the region to the north. Further road cut checks could prove worthwhile.

Site 30 Fossils at Storrie Lake

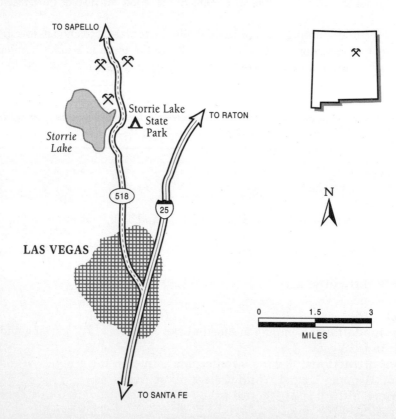

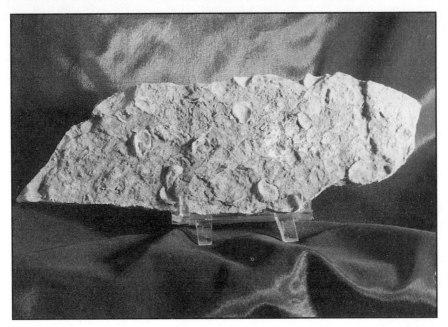

Slabs of Pierre shale present ideal collecting of marine fossils.

SITE 31 *GRAVELS NEAR CONCHAS LAKE*

Land type: Rolling plains.
Elevation: 4,000 feet.
Best season: Any.
Land manager: New Mexico State Highway and Transportation Department.
Material type: Rocks for tumbling.
Material: Hematite, agate, jasper, petrified wood.
Level of difficulty: Moderate.
Tools: None.
Vehicle: Any.
Accommodations: Motel and RV parking at Conchas Lake.
Special attractions: Fishing, boating.
For more information: Conchas Lake State Park 505-868-2270.
Finding the site: Conchas Lake is located on New Mexico Highway 104 northwest of Tucumcari. From Tucumcari take NM 104 north about 17.6 miles. Look for the sandy, gravel-bearing roadcuts west of milepost 88.

Rockhounding: Wanted: One stop shopping for rocks suitable for tumbling. Seeking colorful agate, jasper, and flint, hematite, quartzite, well agatized wood and maybe even an opal or two.

Site 31 Gravels Near Conchas Lake

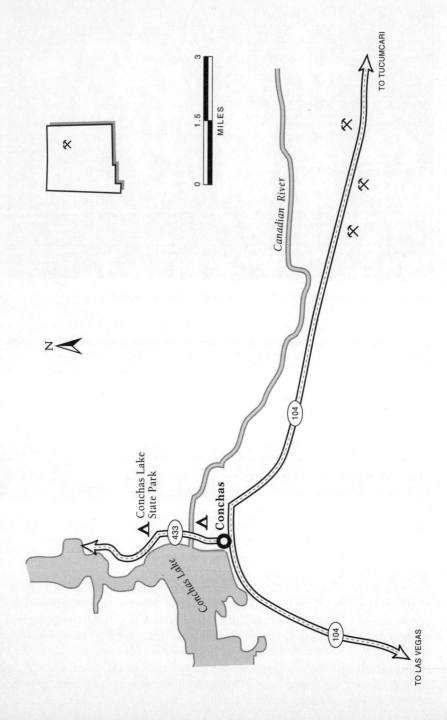

Composed of gravels washed here from the Rockies, then capped by sun-baked caliche, the Ogallala formation has all of that to offer and much more. These gravel beds overlie much of the Texas Panhandle and extend into New Mexico to just west of Tucumcari. The nearby Canadian River aided in exposing these beds in the road cuts along NM 104.

The specimens here are surprisingly not as travel-worn as those found in the Ogallala beds elsewhere. Look for warm brown jasper, flint similar to the famous Alibates flint found near Amarillo, and slivers of what is known as Canadian River red agate. The pieces are small but brilliant, with red, white, and gold banding.

Opal has reportedly been found in the "breaks" of the Canadian River and in the Ogallala formation throughout Quay County. Keep in mind, however, that opal dries rather quickly when exposed to extreme weather. If that is the treasure you seek, take along a shovel and be prepared to dig below the freeze line. That is also good advice if you are interested in flint that you intend to work. The freeze-thaw cycles cause the flint to become highly fractured.

Conchas Lake State Park is high on New Mexico's list of great recreation spots. The park offers lakeside camping, including many sites with full hook-ups and shelters, as well as hotel accommodations for those without RVs.

SITE 32 *FOSSILS AND PETRIFIED WOOD NEAR LOGAN*

Land type: Hills.
Elevation: 3,900 feet.
Best season: Spring, fall.
Land manager: New Mexico State Highway and Transportation Department.
Material type: Loose fossils.
Material: Cretaceous fossils, petrified wood.
Level of difficulty: Moderate.
Tools: None.
Vehicle: Any.
Accommodations: Camping at Ute Lake State Park.
Special attraction: Fishing.
For more information: Ute Lake State Park 505-487-2284.
Finding the site: Logan is located on the shores of Ute Lake about 24 miles northeast of Tucumcari. From Logan take U.S. Highway 54 about 1.8 miles south to the junction with New Mexico Highway 469. Turn east. About 1.7 miles after turning, the road crosses Revuelto Creek. Look for fossils in the road cuts near the river.

Rockhounding: This is one of the few places in the state where marine fossils can be obtained free from a tough matrix material. Finds are generally bivalves ranging in size from 0.5 to 1 inch across. They are scattered throughout the caliche near Revuelto Creek.

Look for the petrified wood here, as well as in the "breaks" of the Canadian River. Pieces are usually small but well agatized. Occasional slivers of flint, jasper, and agate occur in these same areas. Wood litters the shores of Ute Lake, but because the lake is part of the state park, no collecting is allowed there.

Site 32 Fossils and Petrified Wood Near Logan

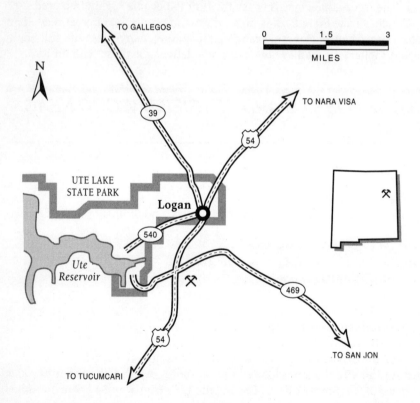

SITE 33 *WOOD AND AGATE NEAR BERNARDO*

Land type: Hills.
Elevation: 4,700 feet.
Best season: Any.
Land manager: New Mexico State Highway and Transportation Department.
Material type: Rocks for cutting and polishing.
Material: Petrified wood, agate.
Level of difficulty: Moderate.
Tools: Shovel, rake.
Vehicle: Any.
Accommodations: Motels and RV parks in either Socorro or Albuquerque.
Special attractions: Bernardo Wildlife Area 505-864-8136.
Finding the site: Bernardo is located off of Interstate Highway 25 between Albuquerque and Socorro. From I-25 travel 2.1 miles on U.S. Highway 60 to the Rio Grande bridge. Cross the bridge, then turn north onto a dirt road.

Site 33 Wood and Agate Near Bernardo

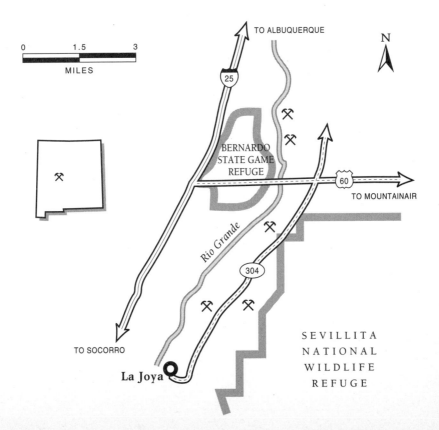

Collecting is possible along this dirt road. Also try traveling an additional 0.5 miles east of the bridge to New Mexico Highway 304. Turn south. Search the roadsides and washes that cross the road. Good collecting continues for more than 6 miles.

Rockhounding: There are very few places in the state where wood of this quality can be collected. The colors include black, brown, white, and deep red. Every piece is either well agatized or opalized. The only problem is that this area has been known for years and surface material is minimal. The best examples are usually found by raking the upper layers of topsoil or even digging small trenches. Digging is the only way to retrieve the truly opalized pieces anyway.

Both agatized and opalized woods form as the result of silica replacement of the organic material in the wood. The difference between the two is water. Agate is a variety of chalcedony, which is nothing more than microcrystalline quartz. The chemical composition is silicon dioxide (SiO_2). Opal is hydrous silica ($SiO_2 \bullet nH_2O$). When exposed to weather extremes, the water in opal evaporates, leaving the silicon dioxide or simply agate. To get to the pieces that are not dried out you've got to break out the shovel. Just remember to fill in any holes you dig.

The agate here is sparse, but worth keeping a lookout for. The pieces are usually small, but make excellent tumbling material. The primary colors are black and clear, with random swirls. There are some pebbles of jasper here as well.

SITE 34 *FLUORITE AND MINERALS AT THE BLANCHARD MINES*

Land type: Mountains.
Elevation: 4,800 feet.
Best season: Fall.
Land manager: Blanchard Rock Shop.
Material type: Gemstones, mineral specimens, rocks for tumbling.
Material: Fluorite, barite, galena, linarite, quartz, chrysocolla, brochantite.
Level of difficulty: Easy to moderate.
Tools: Shovel, pick, hammer, safety glasses, packing material and containers, detail tools like ice picks and small brushes.
Vehicle: Any.
Accommodations: Motels and RV parking in either Socorro or Carrizozo; camping at Valley of Fires National Recreation Site.
Special attractions: Mineral display at New Mexico Institute of Mining and Technology.
For more information: New Mexico Institute 505-835-5420; Valley of Fires 505-624-1790.
Finding the site: The Blanchard Mines are located south of what is left of

Perfect fluorite cubes are just one of the prizes found at the Blanchard mines.

the town of Bingham on U.S. Highway 380, 28 miles east of Interstate Highway 25 and 35 miles west of Carrizozo. The Blanchard Rock Shop is on US 380. Stop here to pay the collecting fee and get directions to the mine dumps.

Rockhounding: If there is one site in New Mexico that can make you fall in love with minerals, this is it. Don't make this the first place you collect in this state, or you may never see the rest. I met a hound here from Colorado who had been coming here for six years and had never even visited the Kelly Mining District, just 60 miles away.

The most important tool to take along to the Blanchard Claims is knowledge. Know what is here, what it looks like, and its geological habits. The information provided here is meant to be a brief primer to get you started, and a stop at the Mineral Museum at New Mexico Institute in Socorro is also advisable prior to collecting at Bingham.

The Blanchard claims are a part of the Hansonberg Mining District, named for Colonel A.H. Hanson. The claims originally consisted of seven mines. Collecting is now limited entirely to above-ground workings and dumps. The fee at time of publication was five dollars per day per person, and each person must sign a waiver.

The biggest drawing card here is undoubtedly the fluorite. Museum-quality specimens are immanently possible. Perfect, cubic crystals are abundant in colors that include clear, blue, blue green, pale green, violet, and deep purple. The cubes range in size from microscopic to more than 3 inches. Some of the prettiest are bedded on calcite, quartz, and barite.

The fluorite forms in several stages, which accounts for the color variations. The purples and blues are rarely found together, but both occur in crevices and faults in the limestone. Two methods of recovery can be used. One procedure is to break open the abundant limestone rocks, searching for crystal-lined crevices. The second involves finding a faulted area in the hillside itself and carefully digging away the granular rock. This should be a slow, meticulous process using an ice pick or screwdriver to explore possible cracks.

Obviously both methods are time consuming and labor intensive. The casual collector may wish to simply search the rubble left behind by others. This can prove quite fruitful, because many collectors quickly become jaded by the beauty found here and leave behind specimens that are only slightly less than spectacular.

In addition to the fluorites, there is a long list of other minerals to seek. Linarite, which is a brilliant blue, is usually found on calcite or gypsum. Radiating crystal groups more than 1 inch high have been found in the tunnels here, but the chief finds today are flat sprays or patches. Even these are extraordinary. Also look for green minerals like brochantite, usually found in crystalline masses, malachite as tiny opaque inclusions, and chrysocolla.

There is a simple method of sorting out the chrysocolla from the other green, or even blue minerals. The chrysocolla will turn olive green and eventually even black as the result of oxidation. This color change can be acceler-

The view from the hillside workings of the Blanchard mines isn't much of a distraction from the treasure.

ated using hydrogen peroxide. A light blue green piece will begin to oxidize and darken almost immediately.

Galena is abundant. Because it is a cavity-filling mineral, look for cubes in the same places as the fluorite. They are often found together. Galena was the primary lead source mined in this district. My grandfather once spent several years mining here, bringing home buckets full of the cubes. By all accounts he hauled in enough to thoroughly confuse any future geologist who stumbles upon them on his property in the flatlands of Texas.

SITE 35 *IRON MINERALS AT JONES CAMP*

Land type: Hills.
Elevation: 5,000 feet.
Best season: Summer.
Land manager: Bureau of Land Management.
Material type: Mineral specimens.
Material: Magnetite, titanite, actinolite.
Level of difficulty: Moderate.
Tools: None.
Vehicle: Utility.
Accommodations: Motels and RV parking in either Socorro or Carrizozo; camping at Valley of Fires National Recreation Site.
Special attractions: None.
For more information: Valley of Fires 505-624-1790.

Site 34 Fluorite and Minerals at the Blanchard Mines & Site 35 Iron Minerals at Jones Camp

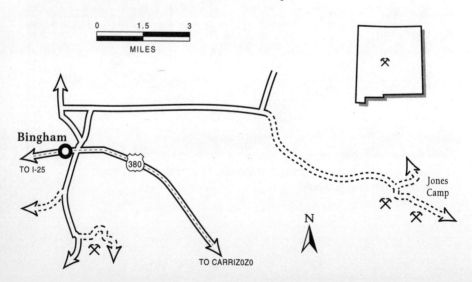

Jones Camp mining district is located in an isolated valley.

Finding the site: The Jones Camp Iron Mines are located northeast of what remains of the town of Bingham, which is located on U.S. Highway 380 28 miles east of Interstate Highway 25, or 35 miles west of Carrizozo. At Bingham turn onto the dirt road heading north. Stay on this road as it turns east toward the mesa. At about 7.5 miles the main road turns back north and a less-traveled road continues east through an unlocked gate. (Be sure to close it behind you.) Travel another 6.7 miles to the mine dumps.

Rockhounding: This is a site that will probably interest only micro-mount mineral collectors, although large specimens of magnetite are abundant here. Most of it is coarse textured, but careful searching turns up a more desirable smooth, metallic surface.

The mounds of green rock found at the eastern end of the district take their color from two sources: tiny green crystals of titanite and granular green actinolite. Crystalline actinolite specimens are also possible. Look for radial fibrous or bladed crystals, sometimes replaced by secondary minerals.

Valley of Fires National Recreation Site offers a rare opportunity to camp or picnic in the middle of a basalt lava flow. The flow came from Little Black Peak, about 7 miles northwest of the park. The flow is about 44 miles long, but only a few miles wide.

Because it is only about 1,000 years old, it presents an opportunity for an up-close look at an almost unchanged flow. The surface is often crinkled and oozy looking, as if it had cooled only yesterday.

The campground has restrooms but no showers, sites with electrical hook-ups, and a trailer dump station. There is a visitor center and self-guided trails across the lava flow. Watch for desert flora and fauna that have made the flow home. Many of the small animals found here will have darker-than-usual coats to help them blend with the dark brown basalt.

SITE 36 *PSILOMELANE NEAR SOCORRO*

Land type: Mountains.
Elevation: 5,000 feet.
Best season: Summer.
Land manager: Bureau of Land Management.
Material type: Rocks for cutting and polishing, mineral specimens.
Material: Manganese oxides.
Level of difficulty: Easy.
Tools: None.
Vehicle: Utility.
Accommodations: Motels and RV parking in Socorro; camping in Cibola National Forest.
Special attraction: Mineral display at New Mexico Institute of Mining and Technology; rock climbing.

Look for the concentric rings that are the tell-tale markings of manganese oxides.

Site 36 Psilomelane Near Socorro

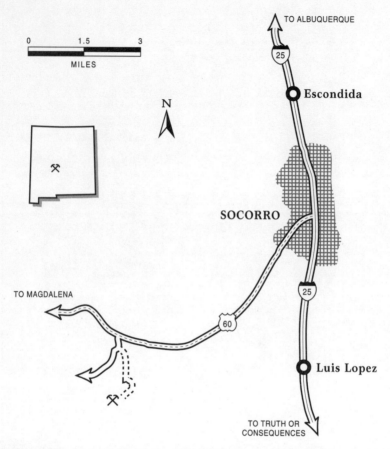

For more information: New Mexico Institute 505-835-5420, Cibola National Forest Magdalena District 505-854-2281.

Finding the site: Socorro is located on Interstate Highway 25 south of Albuquerque. From Socorro take U.S. Highway 60 west for about 7 miles. Turn south on a dirt road that leads into the nearby Chupadera Mountains. At about 0.5 miles, the road splits. Take the left fork into the mountains. There is a gate about 1.3 miles after the split. (Be sure to close it behind you.) Look for the mine dumps about 0.25 miles past the gate.

Rockhounding: Though manganese oxides occur abundantly throughout Socorro County, this abandoned mine site offers one of the best selections of psilomelane specimens. Large massive pieces are abundant in the dumps. Look for the concentric rings of alternating black and silvery black in fractured pieces. This is indicative of the botryoidal pattern common to these minerals.

The sooty black powder on most of the specimens is actually pyrolusite, which is also a manganese ore. Psilomelane streaks black, but rarely is as messy as the pyrolusite, so look for specimens with the least amount of residue.

Psilomelane is fast becoming a trendy mineral among rockhounds. It has been called "black hematite" due to its resemblance of the iron-based mineral when polished. Though generally softer than hematite, it takes a very nice polish. Be forewarned that working with psilomelane is very messy. It produces a greasy black residue that stains skin, clothing, and working surfaces.

The vehicle requirement for this site was listed as utility because the road is very rutted. Most any vehicle with moderately high clearance and good shocks will manage to cover the short distances, provided the road is dry. Do not attempt this road in anything other than four-wheel-drive if there are signs of mud. There is room to park off the road at the first split if you choose to hike the last mile and a half. It is uphill, but would make a pleasant hike.

SITE 37 *MINERALS AT WATER CANYON*

Land type: Mountains.
Elevation: 7,000 feet.
Best season: Summer.
Land manager: USDA Forest Service.
Material type: Mineral specimens.
Material: Manganese oxides, barite, pyrite, calcite.
Level of difficulty: Difficult.
Tools: Shovel.
Vehicle: Four-wheel-drive.
Accommodations: Motels and RV parking in Socorro; camping in Water Canyon.
Special attractions: Camping and hiking.
For more information: Cibola National Forest Magdalena District 505-854-2281.
Finding the site: Water Canyon is located about 14 miles west of Socorro on U.S. Highway 60. Near milepost 124 look for the road to the Water Canyon Campground. Turn south. At about 4.7 miles the road splits. Take the road on the right, which is Forest Service Road 406. (The road to the left goes through the campground.) FR 406 splits at about 0.3 miles. Turn right onto FR 39. At times this road is nothing more than the creek bed. At about 1.7 miles, the creekbed veers off to the right of the road. Turn off of the road and follow the creekbed as far as your vehicle will allow (probably less than 0.25 miles), then continue on foot. A prospect pit will be seen at creekbed level on the right. The lower mine adit is a short hike up from there, and the upper adit is farther up the mountain.

Rockhounding: Micromounters start your engines! This site should satisfy the adventurer lurking within. The difficult rating on this site is based on both the laborious trek to the site and the formidable task of finding specimens.

That said, here's what could be lurking in those tailings piles: anglesite, aragonite, barite (lots of this), calcite (some with black manganese banding), cerussite, galena, hematite, jarosite, mimetite, psilomelane, pyrite (lots of nice coatings), and rose quartz. All except the calcite and pyrite are likely to be found only on micro-mount scale.

The camping facilities at Water Canyon are bare minimum, with no hook-ups or fresh water facilities, but it is a beautiful place to rough it. If the trailer campground is full or not to your liking, drive through it and up the road toward Langmuir Laboratory. There are several nice roadside spots suitable for small trailers or tents.

This area requires bear-avoidance camping. If you are in a tent or canvas-sided trailer, keep no food or toiletries inside with you. These should be locked in your vehicle. The same applies to trash.

Site 37 Minerals at Water Canyon

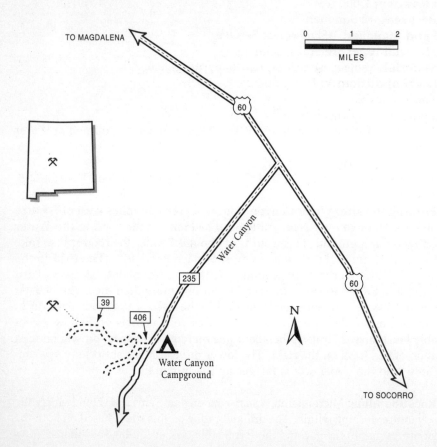

Both upper and lower adits of this mine in Water Canyon are open, but enter at your own risk.

SITE 38 *COPPER MINERALS AT THE KELLY MINE*

Land type: Mountains.
Elevation: 6,000 feet.
Best season: Summer, fall.
Land manager: Tony Otero.
Material type: Gemstones, mineral specimens, rocks for cutting and polishing.
Material: Smithsonite, malachite, azurite, chrysocolla, pyrite, quartz.
Level of difficulty: Moderate.
Tools: Shovels.

Vehicle: Any.

Accommodations: Motels in Magdalena; camping in Cibola National Forest.

Special attraction: Tony's Gems and Minerals 505-854-2401.

For more information: Cibola National Forest Magdalena District 505-854-2281.

Finding the site: The Kelly Mine is located in the hills above the town of Magdalena, which is on U.S. Highway 60 about 27 miles west of Socorro. In Magdalena turn south on Poplar Street. Travel about 0.5 miles to Tony's Gems and Minerals. Stop here to pay the collecting fee, get the gate key, and directions to the mine.

Rockhounding: This a real pain in the neck site, meaning your neck will likely suffer from constantly looking at the ground. You simply cannot take your eyes off the ground here. One blink or stretch skyward could mean missing a gem-quality specimen of smithsonite or a tiny nodule of azurite.

The best means of searching the vast dumps surrounding the famous Kelly Mine is simply to find a spot with surface color, then sit down and carefully sift through the top few inches. One such session could leave you in possession of the following as it did for me: two dime-sized smithsonite specimens, two pieces of azurite, one golf ball-sized chunk of pyrite with nice cubes on one face, one very interesting chrysocolla pseudomorph after linarite, four slivers of malachite, one micro-mount cuprite specimen, and one rock bearing both smoky and citrine varieties of quartz.

There are more than sixty minerals that have been identified at the Kelly. A stop in Socorro at the mineral museum at the New Mexico Institute of Mining and Technology will help expand both your knowledge of the region and your

Site 38 Copper Minerals at the Kelly Mine

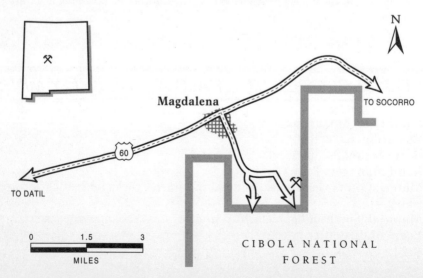

taste for collecting. The museum boasts the most complete and diverse collection of New Mexico minerals in existence. The specimens of azurite and smithsonite from the Kelly will take your breath away.

Collecting status at the Kelly could possibly change in the near future. The claim has been purchased by a California company that reportedly is interested in turning over the dumps, but it is unclear if collecting would be allowed. Tony Otero at the rock shop can advise on the current status of the Kelly and other mines in the district.

The dumps at the Kelly mine offer some of the best mineral collecting in the state.

SITE 39 *AGATE IN TULAROSA CANYON*

Land type: Hills.
Elevation: 6,853 feet.
Best season: Summer.
Land manager: USDA Forest Service.
Material type: Rocks for cutting and polishing.
Material: Agate, chalcedony.
Level of difficulty: Moderate to difficult.
Tools: Rake.
Vehicle: Any.
Accommodations: Motel in Reserve.
Special attractions: None.
For more information: Gila National Forest Reserve Ranger District 505-533-6231.
Finding the site: Tularosa Canyon is located in the Gila National Forest just off of New Mexico Highway 12, between Aragon and Horse Springs. Look for an unmarked dirt road leading south from NM 12, about 6.5 miles east of Aragon. You can begin collecting off of the road anywhere after turning off NM 12.

Rockhounding: Spend some time exploring the sandy plains leading into Tularosa Canyon. You'll likely find some of the best agate and chalcedony the entire area has to offer. Most of the agate here is clear with white fortification banding. Keep a sharp watch for the few pieces scattered around that are clear with red banding or swirls. They are the real prizes.

I was unable to determine the source of the agate, but was told that there are nodules found in the mountain side somewhere near Patterson Peak, which is south of this canyon. That theory seems reasonable since many of the pieces found here are whole or almost whole nodules. Few of them exhibit smooth exteriors, so it is doubtful that they travel far to get here.

Additionally, there is very little agate found east of here, but the agate field continues to the west through Reserve and San Francisco, with elevations gradually dropping as you move west.

The best pieces are at or near the surface and can be unearthed by light raking. Be sure to walk across any area you search in at least two directions to get the best play of light on the rocks. Prime lighting conditions are early and late in the day when the sun is at a lesser angle to the ground. Midday agate hunting is not usually as productive.

Site 39 Agate in Tularosa Canyon & Site 40 Agate Near Aragon & Site 41 Agate Near Apache Creek

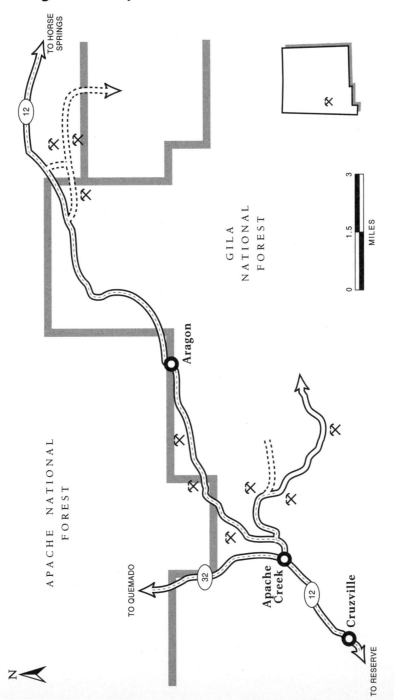

SITE 40 *AGATE NEAR ARAGON*

Land type: Hills.
Elevation: 6,679 feet.
Best season: Summer.
Land manager: USDA Forest Service.
Material type: Rocks for tumbling.
Material: Agate, chalcedony.
Level of difficulty: Easy.
Tools: None.
Vehicle: Any.
Accommodations: Motel in Reserve.
Special attractions: None.
For more information: Gila National Forest Reserve Ranger District 505-533-6231.
Finding the site: Aragon is located in the northern Gila National Forest on New Mexico Highway 12 between Apache Creek and Horse Springs. Search the sandy road cuts along NM 12 between Aragon and Apache Creek.

Rockhounding: Suppose you just happen to be passing through this sleepy valley and don't have time to do any real off-road collecting. This site is for you. The road cuts between Aragon and Apache Creek provide a nice sampling of what abounds in the area.

The agate is usually clear with white fortification banding. Occasional pieces exhibit bright orange red banding. The chalcedony is typical of what is scattered throughout the Gila: white, some with an obvious botryoidal surface. Some of it fluoresces green under short wave ultraviolet light.

SITE 41 *AGATE NEAR APACHE CREEK*

Land type: Hills.
Elevation: 6,409 feet.
Best season: Summer.
Land manager: USDA Forest Service.
Material type: Rocks for cutting and polishing.
Material: Agate, chalcedony.
Level of difficulty: Moderate.
Tools: Rake.
Vehicle: Any.
Accommodations: Motel in Reserve.
For more information: Gila National Forest Reserve Ranger District 505-533-6231.
Finding the site: Apache Creek is located in the Northern Gila National

Forest at the junction of New Mexico Highway 32 and NM 12. From that junction travel 0.75 miles east on NM 12 to a Forest Service Road leading to the southeast into Sand Canyon. This road parallels a creekbed. Search in this dry wash.

Rockhounding: Apache Creek is essentially the center of the agate field that stretches east and west, paralleling NM 12. Agate hunters have been collecting around Apache Creek for years, leaving some areas quite picked over. The streambeds criss-crossing Sand Canyon are still rather productive, though.

The agate is almost all clear with white fortification banding. Sizes range from pea to golf ball. Most are broken pieces, but an occasional whole nodule is possible. Walk the streambed in two directions. If surface collecting doesn't turn up a few good specimens, try lightly raking the conglomeration of river rocks to expose fresh material. Water is also helpful, if you have plenty to spare. The agates are easier to pick out of the pile when wet, especially if they have any red coloring.

Regardless of your own luck in the area, some fine examples of Apache Creek agate can be seen (and purchased) at the Blanchard Rock Shop in Bingham. Obviously it's a considerable distance to drive (158 miles) just for that purpose, but if you plan a trip to collect at the mines there, don't forget to ask them to show you their Apache Creek agates.

SITE 42 *AGATE NEAR RESERVE*

Land type: Hills.
Elevation: 6,206 feet.
Best season: Summer.
Land manager: USDA Forest Service.
Material type: Rocks for cutting and polishing.
Material: Agate, chalcedony.
Level of difficulty: Moderate.
Tools: Rake.
Vehicle: Any.
Accommodations: Motel in Reserve.
Special attractions: None.
For more information: Gila National Forest Reserve Ranger District 505-533-6231.
Finding the site: Reserve is located in the northern Gila National Forest on New Mexico Highway 12, about 8 miles east of U.S. Highway 180. From Reserve take NM 12 northeast for about 5 miles. Turn north onto Forest Service Road 49 to Toriette Lake. The road immediately crosses a streambed that is ideal for collecting.

Rockhounding: Any streambed in this region is a good prospect for agate collecting. This one is no exception. Look for clear and white pieces mixed with

Site 42 Agate Near Reserve &
Site 43 Agate Near San Francisco

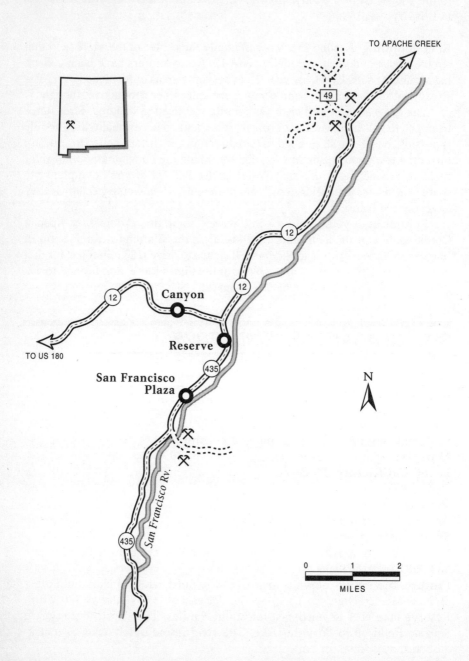

TO APACHE CREEK

49

12

12

Canyon

12

TO US 180

Reserve

435

San Francisco
Plaza

N

San Francisco Rv.

435

0   1   2

MILES

the other river rocks. Patient searching can turn up a mixture of specimens that range in size from tiny slivers to golf-ball sized nodules.

The plain white chalcedony is not as plentiful here as in areas farther up hill and to the east. Additionally, a few agates bearing gray and even black markings can be found here, indicating an additional source.

This area where the Gila and Apache national forests come together is one of the most quietly beautiful in the state. Population levels are low, as is tourist traffic. Unfortunately that makes accommodations somewhat difficult to find. There are a few remote camping areas, but the nearest established campground is Pueblo Park, which has only seven sites. It is located 7 miles off US 180. Commercial RV parks and motel rooms are equally scarce.

SITE 43 *AGATE NEAR SAN FRANCISCO*

Land type: Hills.
Elevation: 5,749 feet.
Best season: Summer.
Land manager: USDA Forest Service.
Material type: Rocks for cutting and polishing.
Material: Agate, chalcedony.
Level of difficulty: Easy.
Tools: None.
Vehicle: Any.
Accommodations: Motel in Reserve.
Special attractions: None.
For more information: Gila National Forest Reserve Ranger District 505-533-6231.
Finding the site: San Francisco is located in the northern Gila National Forest on New Mexico Highway 435 1 mile south of Reserve. Traveling through San Francisco on NM 435, look for the dirt road east to Negrito Creek. The creek parallels the road, but the collecting site is along the banks of the San Francisco River, which the road crosses 0.3 miles from the highway.

Rockhounding: The material collected along the banks of the San Francisco River is a nice mixture of the clear and white agate found to the east and the more colorful agate found near Luna. Look for pieces bearing black, brown, or gray markings. Sometimes the color is in fortification banding and sometimes it occurs as swirls of color.

The chalcedony is scarce, but small pieces are possible, usually stuck in muddy sand bars in the river. If the weather is warm, spend some time searching in the river itself. Lightly disturb the surface rocks, looking for flashes of color that might indicate agate. The pieces with black markings are easy to find, both in the water and out.

SITE 44 *AGATE NEAR RANCHO GRANDE ESTATES*

Land type: Hills.
Elevation: 6,387 feet.
Best season: Summer.
Land manager: USDA Forest Service.
Material type: Rocks for cutting and polishing.
Material: Agate, chalcedony, quartz crystals.
Level of difficulty: Moderate to difficult.
Tools: Rake, shovel.
Vehicle: Any.
Accommodations: Motels in Rancho Grande Estates and Reserve.
Special attractions: None.
For more information: Gila National Forest Reserve Ranger District 505-533-6231.
Finding the site: Rancho Grande Estates is located in the northern Gila National Forest near the junction of U.S. Highway 180 and New Mexico Highway 12. From that junction travel north on US 180 toward Luna, about 0.6 miles, then turn southwest on Forest Service Road 33. Good collecting is possible all along this road. Especially try the creekbed that crosses the road at 0.5 miles from the highway.

Rockhounding: This area has been known to rockhounds for years, but the supply seems to be almost endless. There is plenty here to collect, if you have the time to look. The agate generally presents itself as loose float. It can be clear with white fortification lines, gray with black flecks, and even occasional pieces of sky blue.

The chalcedony is white with excellent botryoidal exteriors. Both the agate and chalcedony frequently occur with quartz-lined cavities or crowns of quartz crystals. There have been reports of amethyst crystals found here as well.

Use this site to whet your appetite for the extraordinary material found closer to Luna. The drive through the pass leading up to Luna is a delightful 700-foot climb. If you have a Forest Service map, try searching other roads along the way. Forest Service Road 35 is a good one to try. It branches off of US 180, 5 miles northwest of FR 33 on the right side of the road. There is a gravel-covered hillside about 0.3 miles after turning from US 180. Search the gravel for agates and quartz.

SITE 45 *AGATE NEAR LUNA*

Land type: Mountains.
Elevation: 7,000 feet.
Best season: Summer.
Land manager: USDA Forest Service.
Material type: Rocks for cutting and polishing.
Material: Agate, chalcedony, quartz.
Level of difficulty: Easy.
Tools: Rake, chisels, hammers.
Vehicle: Any.
Accommodations: Motel in Luna.
Special attractions: None.

Site 44 Agate Near Rancho Grande Estates & Site 45 Agate Near Luna

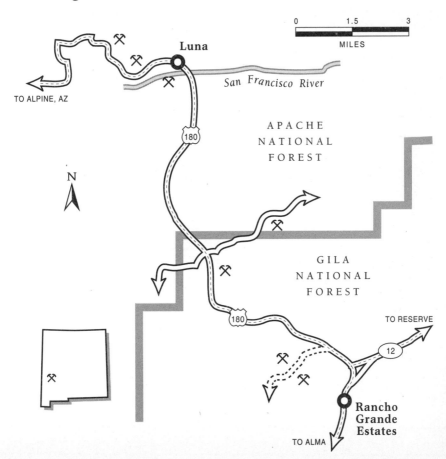

For more information: Gila National Forest Luna Ranger District 505-547-2611.

Finding the site: Luna is located in the Apache National Forest on U.S. Highway 180, about 7 miles from the Arizona border. The agate can be found in all directions from Luna. Try the banks of the San Francisco River and road cuts along US 180 on both sides of town.

Rockhounding: There is almost nothing better than finding agate where it formed, still in place. It's like finally reaching the end of the rainbow. One such place near Luna is found in the road cuts on US 180, about 2.3 miles west of town.

The agate in the cut is clear gray with white fortification banding. The agate surrounds layers of shimmering quartz crystals. It is possible to carefully extract pieces up to 8 or 10 inches long and 2 inches high, that make stunning displays.

After you tire of chipping away at the road cuts, search the Forest Service roads north of town. Almost any of them will lead you to treasure.

Agate and quartz combinations like these are the jewels of the Luna area.

SITE 46 *AGATE AND JASPER NEAR RED HILL*

Land type: High desert.
Elevation: 7,300 feet.
Best season: Spring, fall.
Land manager: Bureau of Land Management.
Material type: Rocks for tumbling (some large enough for cutting.)
Material: Agate, jasper.
Level of difficulty: Difficult.
Tools: Rake.
Vehicle: Utility.
Accommodations: Motel in Quemado.
Special attraction: Very Large Array radio telescope.
For more information: Very Large Array 505-835-7000; Gila National Forest Luna Ranger District 505-547-2611; Quemado Ranger District 505-773-4678.

Site 46 Agate and Jasper Near Red Hill

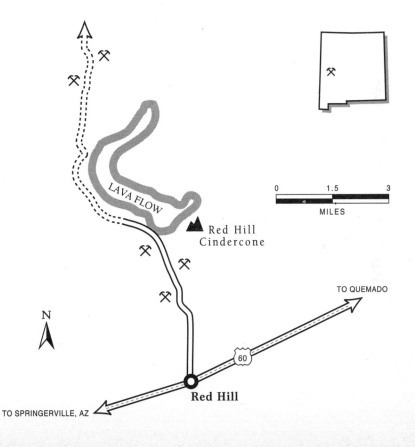

93

The VLA radio telescope is an interesting side trip in this area.

Finding the site: The former town of Red Hill is located roughly 11 miles east of the Arizona border and about 24 miles west of Quemado on U.S. Highway 60. Watch carefully for the remaining buildings. Turn north onto the only road heading in that direction. At about 1.75 miles a side road is marked for the Hall Ranch; stay to the right. Begin looking for the agate and jasper in the road gradings about 1.25 miles farther.

Rockhounding: Agates in black, clear, white, red, and brown are scattered throughout the sandy areas near the Red Hill cinder cone. It is not abundant, but some pieces are quite spectacular. Pebbles of blood red jasper are an added bonus.

The best means of searching is to criss-cross an area from more than one direction. Rake the surface, then look again. Digging may turn up larger pieces, but be careful to refill all holes to avoid injury to cattle.

This is a very remote area, with poorly maintained roads. Unless you happen to be passing through the area, perhaps on your way to Arizona, it may not be worth your time. Also be aware that there are a myriad of dirt roads branching off the main road as it winds its way northward. Unless you have a detailed map, or mark your trail with bread crumbs, do not venture too far.

Seventy-five miles east of Red Hill on US 60 is the VLA National Radio Astronomy Observatory. The VLA consists of twenty-seven dish-shaped antennas which are connected together, creating one large radio telescope. There is a visitor center on site with a slide presentation and details on the operation.

SITE 47 *BYTOWNITE AT PUEBLO PARK CAMPGROUND*

Land type: Mountains.
Elevation: 6,200 feet.
Best season: Summer.
Land manager: USDA Forest Service.
Material type: Gemstones, mineral specimens.
Material: Bytownite, labradorite.
Level of difficulty: Moderate.
Tools: Picks, chisels, hammer.
Vehicle: Any.
Accommodations: Motels in Rancho Grande Estates and Reserve; camping at Pueblo Park Campground.
Special attractions: Camping and hiking.
For more information: Gila National Forest Reserve Ranger District 505-533-6231.
Finding the site: The campground is located in the Apache National Forest, about 6 miles west of U.S. Highway 180. Look for Forest Service Road 232 about 4.5 miles south of the junction of New Mexico Highway 12 and

US 180, or about 21 miles north of the town of Alma. Collecting is in the hills due south of the campground.

Rockhounding: A short hike along the trail leading up to the hills south of this campground can leave you with pocketfuls of tiny treasure. Though the bytownite and labradorite found at Pueblo Park have been known to collectors for years, fine specimens are still abundant. The site's close proximity to the agate fields surrounding Luna and Reserve makes it a worthwhile side trip.

Bytownite and labradorite are members of the plagioclase feldspar group. Their hardness on the Mohs scale is 6, and they leave a white streak. Look for both as loose pieces that have eroded from the surrounding rhyolite and as phenocrysts still embedded in the reddish rhyolite.

Some specimens of the labradorite, though small, are considered gemstone quality due to the play of color found within.

Site 47 Bytownite at Pueblo Park Campground

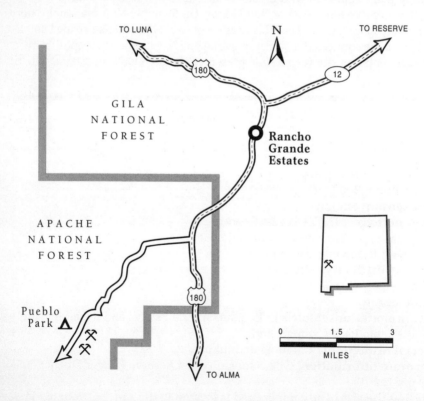

SITE 48 *MINERALS AT MOGOLLON*

Land type: Mountains.
Elevation: 6,996 feet.
Best season: Summer.
Land manager: USDA Forest Service.
Material type: Mineral specimens.
Material: Barite, chrysocolla, quartz.
Level of difficulty: Difficult.
Tools: None.
Vehicle: Any.
Accommodations: Motel in Glenwood; camping in Gila and Apache national forests.
Special attractions: Mogollon ghost town, fishing at Snow Lake.
For more information: Gila National Forest Glenwood Ranger District 505-539-2481;
Finding the site: Mogollon is located on New Mexico Highway 159 in the Gila National Forest, 9 miles east of U.S. Highway 180 and the town of Alma. Collecting is possible on several dumps adjacent to NM 159 and along nearby creek bed and dirt roads.

Main Street in Mogollon.

Rockhounding: At the end of what is perhaps the most crooked paved road in the state lies the tiny village of Mogollon. (Pronounced Mug-e-yon.) As you round the last few curves, the blend of recent mining equipment and antique headframes comes into view. There are a few people visible in town. Two men are visiting on the front porch of the general store. A woman hangs out laundry in the small square of yard that fronts her cottage. If you look closely at the cottage, you can see that it is really one of many connected structures that were probably bunk houses in the old camp days.

There are reminders of the past everywhere you look, from the punched tin facades to the wooden boardwalks. A stop in the dusty general store takes you even further back. Besides the usual assortment of dry goods, there are antique guns, saddles, and of course buckets of rocks.

Because most of the mines and their dumps are located on private property, it isn't likely that you'll find much here to collect. Before you try your luck prowling around the few mines that are accessible, spend some time talking to the locals. Take a moment to fill your mind with images from the past. Those images could very well be the only treasure you need.

If a bit of high-country camping and fishing suits your tastes, stay on NM 159 through Mogollon. There are three campgrounds near one of the region's best trout lakes: Snow Lake. Camping is limited to trailers under 17 feet long and there are only eighteen improved campsites. Primitive camping is allowed as well.

Site 48 Minerals at Mogollon

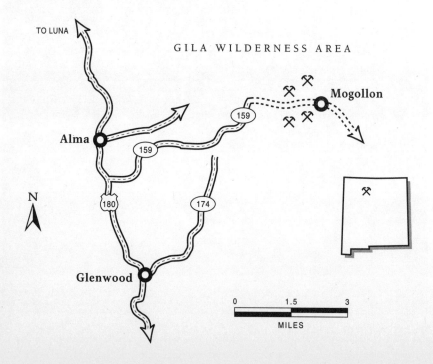

Site 49 Obsidian Near Mule Creek

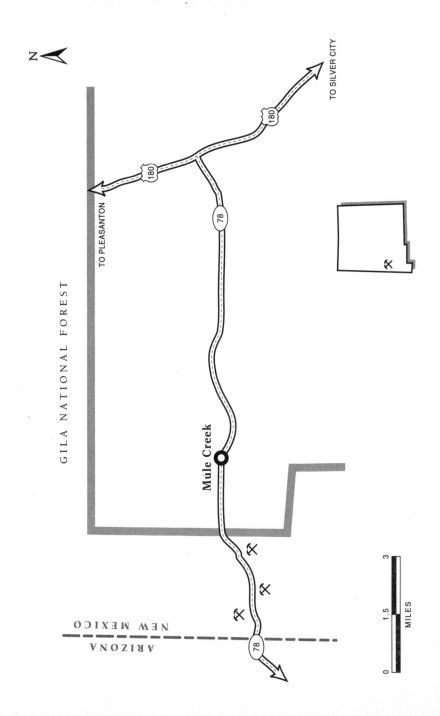

SITE 49 OBSIDIAN NEAR MULE CREEK

Land type: Hills.
Elevation: 5,527 feet.
Best season: Summer.
Land manager: USDA Forest Service.
Material type: Rocks for tumbling.
Material: Obsidian.
Level of difficulty: Easy.
Tools: None.
Vehicle: Any.
Accommodations: Motel in Glenwood.
Special attractions: None.
For more information: Gila National Forest Glenwood Ranger District 505-539-2481.
Finding the site: Mule Creek is located on New Mexico Highway 78 about 9 miles west of U.S. Highway 180. From Mule Creek travel about 3 miles to the Gila National Forest boundary. Collecting is possible along both sides of the road.

Rockhounding: There is sort of an unwritten law in New Mexico that says you should never pass up an opportunity to pick up a few more pieces of obsidian. So if you find yourself traveling along US 180 north of Silver City, take this little side trip to avoid breaking the law.

The obsidian here is generally opaque, but a few tiny droplets are clear enough to be called Apache tears. Careful searching will turn up an occasional piece large enough for cabbing. Raking the sandy surface may be helpful. Don't forget to search with the sun at your back.

SITE 50 ZEOLITES AND CHALCEDONY AT GRAPEVINE CAMPGROUND

Land type: Mountains.
Elevation: 6,483 feet.
Best season: Summer.
Land manager: USDA Forest Service.
Material type: Mineral specimens; rocks for cutting and polishing.
Material: Zeolites, white chalcedony, agate.
Level of difficulty: Moderate.
Tools: Picks, hammers, shovels.
Vehicle: Any.
Accommodations: Motels and RV parking in Silver City; camping in the Gila National Forest.

Zeolites lurk in the basalt rocks lining these banks of the Gila River.

Special attractions: Gila Cliff Dwellings National Monument.

For more information: Gila National Forest Silver City Ranger District 505-538-2271, Wilderness Ranger District 505-536-9461; Silver City Chamber of Commerce 1-800-548-9378. For horseback trips try calling D-Bar Guest Ranch 505-772-5563, Gila Hotsprings Ranch 536-9551, or Gila Wilderness Lodge 772-5772.

Finding the site: Grapevine Campground is located in the Gila National Forest on New Mexico Highway 15, about 36 miles north of Silver City. From Silver City take NM 15 north toward Piños Altos. Continue through Piños Altos via either the historic downtown route or the highway bypass. The campground is about 31 hard miles north.

Rockhounding: Tiny white and pink cubes, patches of stiff gray wool, and fluffy white cotton balls are the minute wonders known as zeolites, found inside the rocks that line the Gila River at Grapevine and Forks campgrounds.

Zeolite is a broad term used to describe a group of hydrous tectosilicate minerals. They are common in some basalts. At Grapevine the basalt rocks are

Site 50 Zeolites and Chalcedony at Grapevine Campground

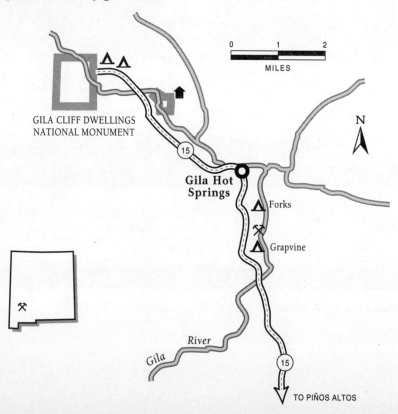

plentiful, as are the zeolites. Museum-quality specimens are possible, even probable. All it takes is plenty of time and energy devoted to splitting the gray and white spotted rocks.

Mixed in with the zeolite-bearing basalt river rocks is an equally plentiful supply of white botryoidal chalcedony. Many pieces are large enough for cutting. There are a few pieces in the mix that qualify more as agate, bearing golden brown fortification lines. Almost all of the chalcedony found here fluoresces green.

The Gila is rich with material for rockhounds to gather. In addition to the zeolites and chalcedony, there are a wide range of agate colors, agate geodes, and petrified wood. Pack trips on horseback can be an ideal way to see more ground and explore areas not accessible by vehicle.

The Grapevine and Forks campgrounds are primitive but beautiful. They make an ideal spot to use as a base camp while exploring the magnificent Gila National Forest. Nearby there are hiking trails, hot springs for soaking your tired feet, and, of course, the cliff dwellings.

As you make the easy hike up to the dwellings, it becomes apparent why this canyon was chosen as home by these people. The beauty is breathtaking. Upon reaching the dwellings that perch 700 feet above the valley, history takes on new meaning. Standing inside the homes of these ancient people, you can almost see the families at work and play, almost hear the whispered wisdom of the elders, almost smell the fires that blackened the high ceilings above. It is truly an experience to savor.

The cliff dwellings are only the beginning of the history that saturates the region. On your way back from there, be sure to stop in at the Buckhorn Saloon (Monday through Saturday after 3 p.m.). This Old West watering hole has been in continuous operation since the mining days of the late 1800s. Ask to see the opera house next door, which offers genuine melodrama presentations on weekends, complete with popcorn to throw and villains to boo.

SITE 51 *COPPER MINERALS IN HANOVER*

Land type: Hills.
Elevation: 5,900 feet.
Best season: Summer.
Land manager: Phelps Dodge Mining Corporation.
Material type: Mineral specimens.
Material: Chrysocolla, malachite.
Level of difficulty: Easy.
Tools: None.
Vehicle: Any.
Accommodations: RV parking and motels in Silver City.
Special attractions: Shopping, sightseeing in Silver City.
For more information: Silver City Chamber of Commerce 1-800-548-9378.

Finding the site: Hanover is located near the junction of New Mexico Highway 152 and NM 356, about 9 miles east of Silver City. From Silver City take U.S. Highway 180 east about 4.5 miles to NM 152. Turn left. Travel 5.8 miles to the overlook into the Chino open pit copper mine. Travel another mile to Phelps Dodge/Chino Santa Rita Park. There are dumps here along the road.

Pictures cannot do justice to the size of the Chino pit mine.

Rockhounding: Massive is an understatement when describing the open pit copper mine known as Santa Rita. Those tiny trucks down in the bottom are capable of carrying upward of 170 tons of ore. When you see it, if you are like most rockhounds, your first reaction will probably be to want a rock from this place. It doesn't even have to be anything spectacular.

To that end, the dump listed above is just the place to get your rock. Most of the rock is leaverite (as in "You oughta leave 'er right there `cause it ain't worth nothin'"), but some contain tiny fragments of malachite and fair amounts of chrysocolla.

Besides, even if the mineral value of these rocks is low, there is a feeling of historical significance related to possessing a piece of the Santa Rita. Not only has copper been mined here since before recorded history, there is the knowledge that just as man created this hole in the ground, man can cover it up.

The area surrounding Silver City is rich in activities. It is advisable that you call ahead for a planning guide published by the Chamber of Commerce. It includes a map, four self-guided tours, and photos and descriptions of some of the best sights to see in the region.

Site 51 Copper Minerals in Hanover

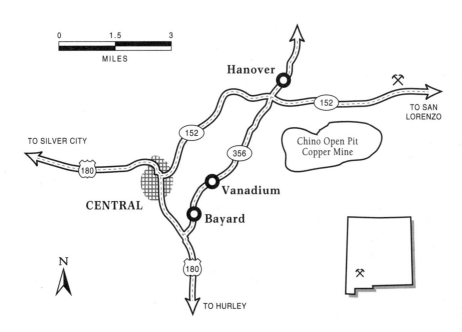

SITE 52 *COPPER MINERALS AT THE TYRONE PIT*

Land type: Hills.
Elevation: 5,600 feet.
Best season: Any.
Land manager: Phelps Dodge Corporation.
Material type: Mineral specimens.
Material: Chrysocolla.
Level of difficulty: Easy.
Tools: None.
Vehicle: Any.
Accommodations: RV parking and motels in Silver City.
Special attractions: Shopping and sightseeing in Silver City.
For more information: Call Phelps Dodge for tour reservations with twenty-four-hour notice, 505-538-5331.
Finding the site: The Tyrone Pit Mine is located just off of New Mexico Highway 90, about 8.6 miles south of Silver City. Collecting is allowed only during tours of the facility. Tours are scheduled for 9 a.m. Monday through Friday. Reservations are required.

Site 52 Copper Minerals at the Tyrone Pit

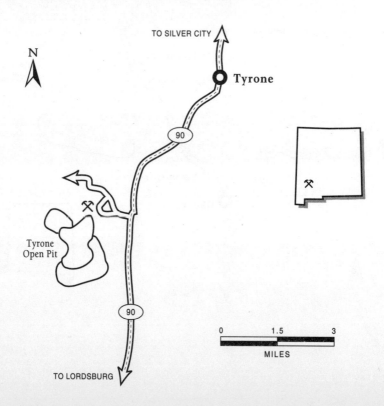

Everything in the Tyrone pit mining operation is on an enormous scale.

Rockhounding: You know what they say, "One person's leaverite is another person's treasure." You may or may not find a rock on the leaverite pile at Tyrone that suits your fancy, but the tour more than makes up for the lack of quality collectibles.

This place is amazing in its ability to squeeze copper from ore that was once considered worthless. By first leaching the copper from ore piled in large dumps, then using an electroplating process, the mine is able to ship out 200-pound sheets of 99.99 percent pure copper.

The mines at Tyrone first went into commercial operation in 1909 when the Phelps Dodge Corporation bought patent claims. Fearing the usual ramshackle mining camp, Mrs. Dodge hired a noted architect to design and build the town of Tyrone, featuring Spanish-style decor. The town was abandoned in 1921 when the original shaft mines closed. The current pit operation began in 1966. As the pit expanded, most of the beautiful ghost town fell to the bulldozers. Only two buildings remain standing. The tour and the rocks from the leaverite pile are free.

SITE 53 *MINERALS AT THE KINGSTON MINES*

Land type: Mountains.
Elevation: 6,519 feet.
Best season: Summer.
Land manager: USDA Forest Service.
Material type: Mineral specimens.
Material: Manganese oxides (manganite, psilomelane), drusy quartz, hemimorphite, rhodochrosite.
Level of difficulty: Moderate.
Tools: Picks, chisels, hammers.

Site 53 Minerals at the Kingston Mines

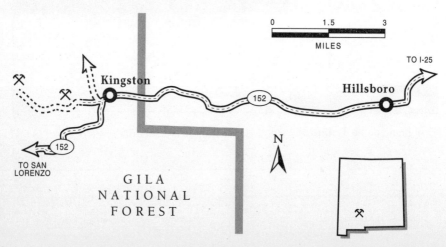

Vehicle: Any.

Accommodations: Bed and breakfasts in Kingston and Hillsboro; camping in Gila National Forest.

Special attractions: Camping, hiking, and fishing.

For more information: Gila National Forest Mimbres Ranger District 505-536-2250.

Finding the site: Kingston is located at the eastern edge of the Gila National Forest on New Mexico Highway 152, between Silver City and Interstate Highway 25. In Kingston take the gravel road west through town. At the end of town, there is a cattleguard, and the road changes to dirt. Due to changing levels of the creek, which crosses the road just past the cattleguard, it may be necessary to hike from here. Stay on the main road for about 0.25 miles. Look for the road up to the mine on your right. The mine and dumps are less than 0.10 miles.

Rockhounding: Besides being in one of the most picturesque settings in the state, the dumps in the Kingston Mining District are viable sources of micromount specimens. The drusy quartz is both beautiful and easily found. Split pieces of the gray rocks bearing quartz and calcite veins, which are scattered throughout the dumps, to find the crystal lined vugs.

The brownish hemimorphite crystals are found in the same manner, but associated with long, gap-tooth calcite crystals. The rhodochrosite is much more difficult to find, but possible in the same rocks. The manganese oxides are very plentiful, but it may take careful digging through the dumps to turn up quality psilomelane specimens.

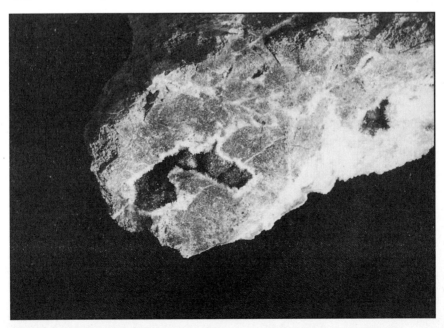

Tiny vugs lined with drusy quartz are common in the Kingston mining district.

SITE 54 *JASPER AND AGATE IN THE CABALLO MOUNTAINS*

Land type: Mountains.
Elevation: 4,000 feet.
Best season: Summer.
Land manager: Bureau of Land Management.
Material type: Rocks for tumbling, cutting, and polishing.
Material: Jasper, agate.
Level of difficulty: Moderate.
Tools: Shovel.
Vehicle: Any.
Accommodations: Camping at Caballo Lake State Park; motels at Truth or Consequences.
Special attraction: Fishing.
For more information: Caballo Lake State Park 505-743-3942.

Site 54 Jasper and Agate in the Caballo Mountains

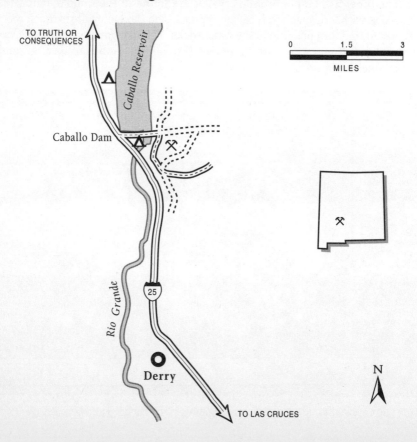

Finding the site: The Caballo Mountains parallel Interstate Highway 25 south of Truth or Consequences. From I-25 take exit 59 to Caballo Lake State Park. Take the road to the right, which is marked "dam access." Cross the dam. At the east end of the dam you will have several choices of dirt roads. Take the road on the far right, marked "river access." Travel about 1.5 miles, following the river. Turn left onto a paved road leading into the hills. Travel 0.5 miles. Look for the pilings of sand and gravel that remain from an abandoned gravel operation.

Rockhounding: Slivers of beer-bottle brown agate mingle here with warm caramel colored and red swirled jasper. Most of the pieces are pebble size, but never overlook the possibility of a larger find. I recovered a beautiful 15 pound chunk of pure, slabbing quality jasper.

This site is an abandoned gravel pit. It pays to first scour the remaining gravel piles, then move on to the source: the dug-out hillsides to the north.

In addition to the agate and jasper, the Caballo Mountains are known for petrified wood, fossils, and carnelian agate. All are possible at or near this location.

The camping facilities at Caballo Lake are excellent for both RVers and rough campers. The campground below the dam is the most up-to-date and is pleasantly set on the banks of the Rio Grande. There are numerous pull-through sites with electricity and water, as well as shaded picnic tables. The location of the lake makes it an ideal base camp for collecting in the Caballos, as well as the eastern edges of the Gila National Forest. The agate fields near Hatch are also only a short drive away.

SITE 55 *CARNELIAN IN THE CABALLO MOUNTAINS*

Land type: Mountains.
Elevation: 4,300 feet.
Best season: Summer.
Land manager: Bureau of Land Management.
Material type: Gemstones, rocks for tumbling.
Material: Carnelian agate, jasper.
Level of difficulty: Very difficult.
Tools: Rake.
Vehicle: Utility or four-wheel-drive.
Accommodations: Motels and RV parking in Truth or Consequences; camping at Elephant Butte or Caballo Lake state parks.
Special attraction: Fishing.
For more information: Elephant Butte State Park 505-744-5421; Caballo Lake State Park 505-743-3942.
Finding the site: The Carnelian is found on the eastern slopes of the mountains, at the southern end of the range. Access from the south is via Interstate Highway 25 near Rincon. Take Exit 32 to Upham south of

Site 55 Carnelian in the Caballo Mountains

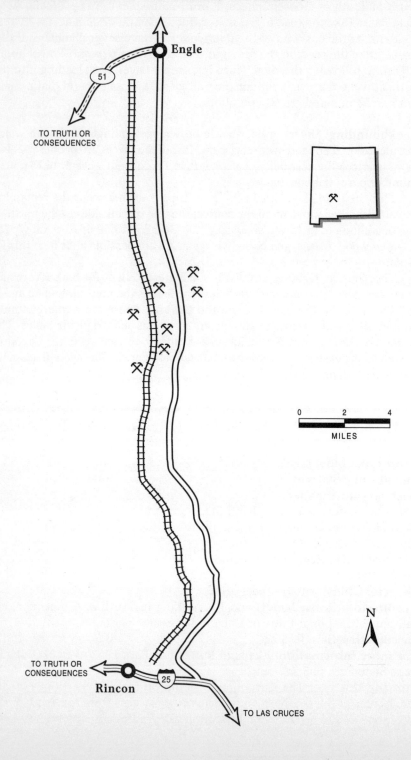

Engle

51

TO TRUTH OR
CONSEQUENCES

0   2   4
MILES

N

TO TRUTH OR
CONSEQUENCES

25

Rincon

TO LAS CRUCES

Rincon. Travel northwest about 1 mile. Turn right at the first fork, then immediately left. This dirt road meets up with a railroad track and parallels it after about 11 miles. Search the washes and road gratings for the next 10 miles. A short hike west toward the mountains could prove fruitful.

Access from the north is through the town of Engle located on New Mexico Highway 51 about 15 miles east of Truth or Consequences. In Engle turn south on the road paralleling the railroad tracks. Travel south about 13 miles, then begin searching the washes and any side roads toward the mountains.

Rockhounding: There is something almost magical about carnelian agate. When you find a piece bearing the soft swirls of orange and red, it can be love at first sight. This is a site reserved for those hardy souls who really love the stuff though. It is one of only a few sites in New Mexico reported to have small quantities of carnelian. Another is the rather famous Cooke's Peak area, which has been all but wiped out. Even after a hard rain, it is almost impossible to find anything but tiny specks.

That is not to say that this site is a whole lot better. But a few hours of hard searching can turn up a handful of small quality pieces. Your chances improve with recent rain. Try not to do your hunting in the middle of a clear day. Overhead sunshine makes the orange almost invisible. Cloudy days present the best collecting opportunity, but keep a watchful eye on those clouds. The dirt road getting here is not too bad when dry, but gets very slippery when wet.

SITE 56 *AGATE AND WOOD NEAR HATCH*

Land type: Hills.
Elevation: 4,055 feet.
Best season: Summer.
Land manager: Bureau of Land Management.
Material type: Rocks for tumbling.
Material: Agate, chalcedony, petrified wood.
Level of difficulty: Moderate.
Tools: Rake.
Vehicle: Utility.
Accommodations: Motel in Hatch.
Special attractions: None.
For more information: Hatch Chamber of Commerce 505-267-5050.
Finding the site: Hatch is located just off of Interstate Highway 25 on New Mexico Highway 26. In Hatch take NM 26 south. Mark mileage at the junction of NM 26 and NM 187 and travel 11.3 miles to County Road 5. Turn left. Take this road straight up the hills, veering right at two forks in the road. Begin collecting after the second fork.

Rockhounding: Ever notice how the best agates are sometimes found in the center of a bone dry, hot, desolate, rattlesnake-infested desert? This place certainly follows that rule. The only green in this area is in the world famous chilies they grow. (Come to think of it, the best chilies are usually grown in a bone-dry, hot, desolate, rattlesnake-infested desert too.)

The agate is similar to that found farther north near Albuquerque. The colors are mostly brown, black, and clear. The bubbly white chalcedony is not quite as plentiful as the agate, but specimens are very nice. The wood is even less plentiful, but is well agatized, and some pieces show interior color. All materials occur in small pieces for the most part. Some digging could conceivably turn up larger chunks.

Opals have been reported in this area as well, but remember that they will generally not be found on the surface. Opal is a hydrous silica; the water can dry rather quickly when exposed to these conditions. If you want the opals, be prepared to dig for them.

Site 56 Agate and Wood Near Hatch

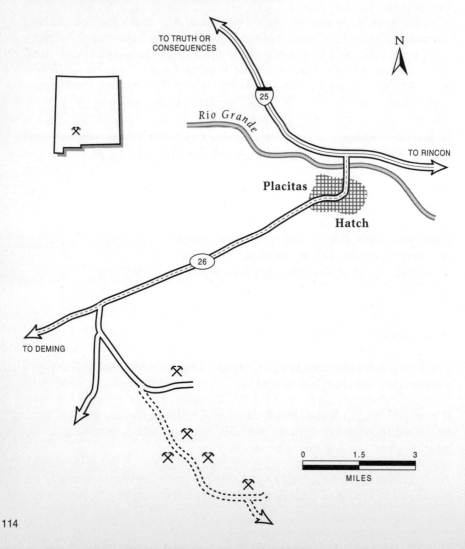

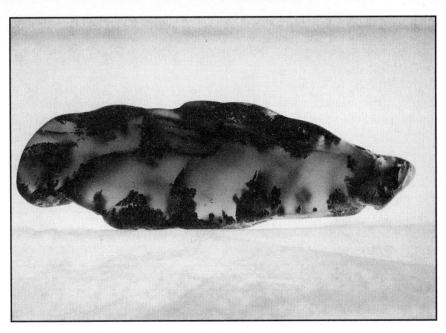

The agate near Hatch is often worth fighting the rattlesnakes to get.

SITE 57 *FLUORITE NORTH OF DEMING*

Land type: Hills.
Elevation: 4,500 feet.
Best season: Summer.
Land manager: Bureau of Land Management.
Material type: Mineral specimens, gemstones.
Material: Fluorite, psilomelane.
Level of difficulty: Moderate.
Tools: Shovel, picks, hammer.
Vehicle: Utility.
Accommodations: RV parking and motels in Deming.
Special attractions: None.
For more information: Deming Tourism Center 505-546-2674.
Finding the site: Deming is located on Interstate Highway 10 between Las Cruces and the Arizona border. In Deming take exit 82A to U.S. Highway 180. Travel north on US 180, 1.2 miles to New Mexico Highway 26. Turn right. Travel 5.1 miles to a dirt road toward the mountains. Turn left. Travel 5.6 miles, crossing four cattleguards, to the mine sites.

Rockhounding: Many hounds come to Deming seeking only the agate and jasper, but this mining district known as Fluorite Ridge has historically produced some of the finest fluorite specimens in all of New Mexico. Numerous examples have been museum quality. There are more than fifteen individual mines or prospect pits. Many still have active claims, so respect any warning signs. Any dumps that are not posted are open to casual, non-commercial collecting. Do not attempt to enter any tunnels.

The fluorite mined here is in several forms, ranging from massive veins to tiny cubic crystals, all of which abound in the dumps. The predominant color is pale green, but some violet is here as well. Some of the best specimens exhibit both principal colors, but these are very difficult to find. Keep in mind that fluorite eventually fades in bright sunlight. Better color may be found below the surface of the dumps.

Some success in obtaining good crystal formations may be achieved by splitting larger stones. Look for the cavities in which the crystals grow.

SITE 58 *PSILOMELANE NORTH OF DEMING*

Land type: Hills.
Elevation: 4,500 feet.
Best season: Summer.
Land manager: Bureau of Land Management.
Material type: Rocks for cutting and polishing.
Material: Psilomelane.
Level of difficulty: Difficult.
Tools: Rake.
Vehicle: Utility.
Accommodations: RV parking and motels in Deming.
Special attractions: None.
For more information: Deming Tourism Center 505-546-2674.
Finding the site: Deming is located on Interstate Highway 10 between Las Cruces and the Arizona border. In Deming take exit 82A to U.S. Highway 180. Travel north on US 180, 1.2 miles to New Mexico Highway 26. Turn right. Travel 5.1 miles to a dirt road toward the mountains. Turn left. Travel north approximately 1.75 miles to a rutted dirt road east. The dumps are 2 miles down this road, in front of the small grouping of hills. Do not attempt to drive this road unless it is dry.

Rockhounding: Really outstanding rocks feel good in your hand, sort of weighty and smooth. These pieces of psilomelane are really outstanding rocks. The heavily botryoidal surface is just icing on the cake. Psilomelane has been called black hematite because it polishes to a deep gray metallic finish. The specimens found here are almost too good to polish, however.

Try collecting a few pieces for working, as well as some that exhibit the best botryoidal formation for display only. You will not find such outstanding specimens anywhere else in the state. In fact, what is generally called psilomelane elsewhere is often a mixture of manganese oxides including pyrolusite. X-ray studies have conclusively identified the material found here as psilomelane, though.

Site 57 Fluorite North of Deming &
Site 58 Psilomelane North of Deming &
Site 59 Agate at Big Diggings&
Site 60 Rockhound State Park

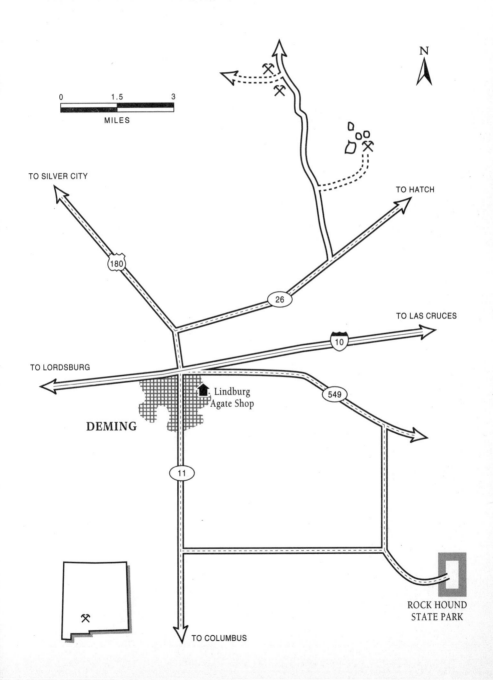

N

0   1.5   3
MILES

TO SILVER CITY

TO HATCH

180

26

TO LAS CRUCES

10

TO LORDSBURG

549

Lindburg
Agate Shop

DEMING

11

ROCK HOUND
STATE PARK

TO COLUMBUS

This site was reportedly a gold dredging operation at one time. The psilomelane was sold off as a byproduct for railroad bedding material for only a few dollars per ton. A claim still exists for the site, but casual collecting is allowed.

If you have never worked with psilomelane, keep in mind that it is extremely messy. Tumbling the smaller pieces works very well, but the slurry will be black and greasy. And it stains, everything. Wear gloves, aprons, and protect working areas with plastic if necessary. Because the material is relatively soft, 80 grit is about as fine as you need to start. Work down through several stages, then finish with ground walnut hulls and washing powder.

This psilomelane specimen needs no enhancing to please most mineral collectors.

SITE 59 *AGATE AT BIG DIGGINGS*

Land type: Hills.
Elevation: 4,300 feet.
Best season: Fall.
Land manager: Lindberg Agate Shop.
Material type: Rocks for cutting and polishing.
Material: Agate.
Level of difficulty: Moderate.
Tools: None.
Vehicle: Any.
Accommodations: RV parking and motels in Deming.
Special attractions: None.
For more information: Deming Tourism Center 505-546-2674.
Finding the site: Deming is located on Interstate Highway 10 between Las Cruces and the Arizona border. In Deming look for the Lindberg Agate Shop just off of I-10 on Country Club Road. Stop here for collecting information. The claim is reached by traveling south on New Mexico Highway 11 about 8.5 miles. Turn west at the school building, continue about 4 miles, then turn south at the stop sign. Go about 6 miles, then turn right again and travel another 6 miles on the dirt road that leads into the heart of the claim. You must return to the Lindberg Agate Shop to weigh in and pay for your material.

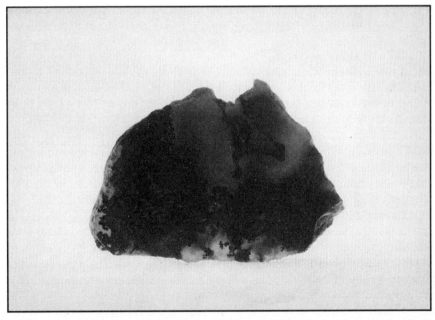

Agates showing both moss inclusions and fortification banding are easily found at Big Diggings.

Rockhounding: There is not a lot that can be said about the agate found at Big Diggings that has not already been said before. The area has been featured in national periodicals and has a worldwide reputation for outstanding agate.

The color range is extraordinary, as is the array of patterns. Obviously since this is a well-known site, it is getting more difficult to find the better pieces. It requires more than a short stroll around the property with your head down. Break out the shovel and rake to get at the good stuff. Plan to take back more than you think you need. The small price per pound is well worth it. How many times have you returned home and really wished you had brought home more of something after you had the chance to clean it up and work on it a little? Don't let that be the case with the Big Diggings agate.

SITE 60 *ROCKHOUND STATE PARK*

Land type: Mountains.
Elevation: 4,700 feet.
Best season: Fall.
Land manager: State of New Mexico.
Material type: Rocks for cutting and polishing.
Material: Jasper.
Level of difficulty: Moderate.
Tools: Rake, picks, chisels, hammer.
Vehicle: Any.
Accommodations: Camping at the park; RV parking and motels in Deming.
Special attractions: None.
For more information: Rockhound State Park 505-546-6182.
Finding the site: Rockhound State Park is located southeast of Deming. In Deming take either New Mexico Highway 549 east or NM 11 south to roads leading to the park.

Rockhounding: Do not expect to go to Rockhound State Park and find examples of the beautiful agate found elsewhere in the region. It won't happen, unless you are an expert climber. The principal low-elevation find in the 300-acre park is some very nice jasper. The agate is a little higher up, about 700 feet. Having said that, enjoy scratching around near the foot of the mountain for the jasper, then move on to some of the outstanding collecting sites elsewhere in the area.

The campground is limited, but was undergoing some renovations at the time of writing. Because Deming is home to many northern visitors and retirees however, the RV accommodations in town are outstanding.

Be sure to stop in at the rock shop just outside the park entrance to see samples of the treasure available in this mineral-rich region. The man who owns the shop does have some agate from inside the park that will either entice you to break out the climbing gear, or open your wallet. It's nice stuff.

SITE 61 *CHALCEDONY AT HERMANAS*

Land type: Hills.
Elevation: 4,500 feet.
Best season: Any.
Land manager: Bureau of Land Management.
Material type: Rocks for cutting and polishing.
Material: Chalcedony, agate.
Level of difficulty: Moderate.
Tools: Rake, water for washing.
Vehicle: Any.
Accommodations: Camping at Pancho Villa State Park; motels and RV parking in Deming.
Special attractions: None.
For more information: Poncho Villa State Park 505-531-2711.
Finding the site: Hermanas is located just north of the Mexican border on New Mexico Highway 9, about 20.4 miles west of Columbus. Collect along the roadside west of the stock pens.

Rockhounding: For roadside collecting, it just doesn't get any better than this. The chalcedony is in pieces large enough to cut and polish, but its form is so spectacular, you may want to just clean it up. Like piles of melted wax, it is highly botryoidal. The predominate colors are clear and snow white, some with droplets of blood red either on the surface or interior. Occasionally the red streaks follow the botryoidal shape and create lovely fortification agate.

The dark splotches on this chalcedony are blood-red.

The prize pieces, though, are a pale pink or lavender. The subtle color will probably not be obvious under the bright sun. Some on-site washing may help, as will viewing in the shade of your vehicle.

Good specimens can be found on both sides of the road. Look at the ground where vegetation is sparse. Surface collecting is excellent, but a light raking should improve your odds of finding larger pieces.

If you need a place to camp for the night, Pancho Villa State Park is probably the most unusual park in the state. The campground is heavily planted with succulents, giving it a true Southwestern feel. The park marks the site where the Mexican Revolution spilled across the border when General Pancho Villa attacked the U.S. Army stationed near Columbus. It was the last time the United States was attacked by a foreign power and the first time air power and mechanical vehicles were used in its defense.

Finally, this is rattlesnake heaven! Collect with one eye looking for rocks and the other looking for snakes. Carry a stick to stir up the brush in front of you, and NEVER reach down to pick up a rock without first scanning the area for snakes.

Site 61 Chalcedony at Hermanas & Site 62 Thunder Eggs at the Baker Mine

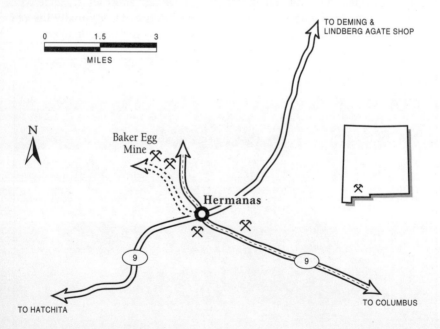

SITE 62 THUNDER EGGS AT THE BAKER MINE

Land type: Hills.
Elevation: 4,500 feet.
Best season: Summer.
Land manager: Lindberg Agate Shop.
Material type: Rocks for cutting and polishing.
Material: Agate, chalcedony.
Level of difficulty: Difficult.
Tools: Shovel, pick, hammer.
Vehicle: Utility.
Accommodations: RV parking and motels in Deming; camping at Pancho Villa State Park.
Special attractions: None.
For more information: Poncho Villa State Park 505-531-2711.
Finding the site: Deming is located on Interstate Highway 10 between Las Cruces and the Arizona border. In Deming look for the Lindberg Agate Shop just off of I-10 on Country Club Road. You must stop here for directions and instructions regarding the electric fence, as well as return to weigh in your goodies.

Rockhounding: The agate thunder eggs found on the Lindberg claims are deep blue alternating with cool rose and green. This soothing combination of colors has a depth and clarity rarely seen in agates found anywhere else. The cool earth tones are sometimes interspersed with bold slashes of white or black. The typical pattern is fortification, but occasional eggs bear only random swirls.

Many of the nodules found here are crystal-lined geodes, rather than the solid agate. These are very nice as well, particularly if they exhibit both the agate lining and the crystals. Rare finds of amethyst crystals lining the interior have been reported.

Spectacular cut and polished examples of the eggs are displayed at the rock shop located near the entrance to Rockhound State Park. Keep in mind, though, that this man makes his living off these eggs and works very hard at finding the best examples. The largest come from inside the mine itself, where he owns the claim. Unfortunately the BLM will not allow him to permit access to others because of the danger involved.

Take heart though, fine small examples are possible in the dumps and throughout this claim area. It may take some digging, but these eggs are worth breaking a sweat over.

SITE 63 *SMELTING SLAG NEAR PLAYAS*

Land type: Plains.
Elevation: 4,390 feet.
Best season: Any.
Land manager: New Mexico State Highway and Transportation Department.
Material type: Rocks for cutting and polishing.
Material: Slag, agate.
Level of difficulty: Easy.
Tools: None.
Vehicle: Any.
Accommodations: Motels and RV parking in either Lordsburg or Deming.
Special attractions: None.
Finding the site: Playas is located in the far southwestern corner of the state on New Mexico Highway 9. The railroad bed containing the slag stretches in both directions from Playas parallel to NM 9.

Rockhounding: Smooth, gray black stones lay shimmering in the sun along this desolate stretch of highway across the "boot heel" of the state. Many present interesting swirls, and almost all pieces contain little glittering hints of copper. Wait a minute. Back the truck up. Slag?! There are those who will undoubtedly think I have spent one too many days in the New Mexico sun for even mentioning this site.

Yes, slag. This is not the kind of stuff you should drive all the way to the end of the state (it sort of looks like the end of the Earth) to get. However, because it is conveniently near some of the best agate and chalcedony found in the state, it is worth taking a look at.

The origin of the material is unknown, but it is the chief component of the remnants of a railbed that dates back to the early 1900s. The slag could have come from the copper smelting operation at Playas, but that is just speculation. Whatever the source, the stuff is really interesting. The color is slightly darker than polished hematite.

Some of the small, smooth pieces can be tumbled using the following method. Start with a short run (8 hours in a vibrating polisher, 24 hours in a standard rolling tumbler) using 600 grit. Follow that with about the same length of time using a good polish grit. Run them through a wash (48 hours vibrating, 72 hours rolling) using extra water and a teaspoon of washing powder and ground walnut hulls mixed together. For the final step, tumble them dry with plastic beads until they achieve the desired finish. The result is a glossy finish without losing the melted metal shape.

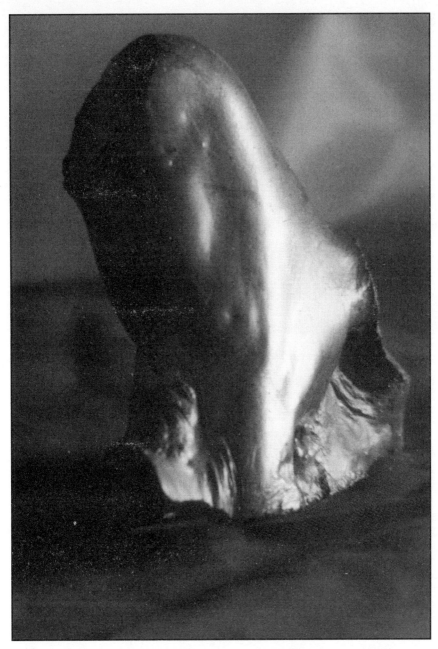

This example of the slag found along the road near Playas has been lightly tumbled to enhance shine, without destroying its character.

Site 63 Smelting Slag Near Playas

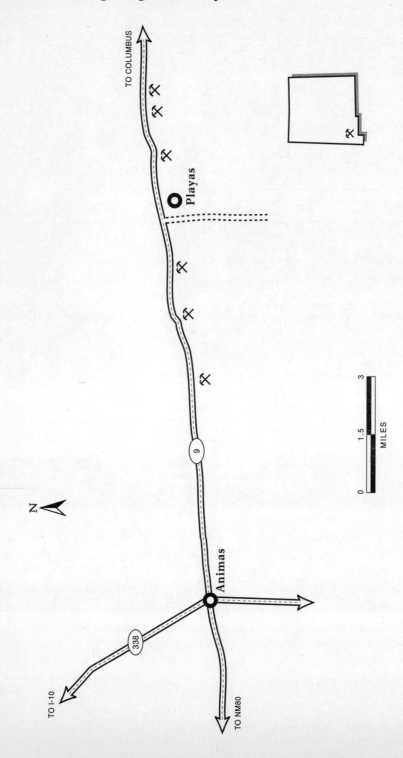

SITE 64 *CHALCEDONY GEODES NEAR ANIMAS*

Land type: Mountains.
Elevation: 5,500 feet.
Best season: Fall.
Land manager: USDA Forest Service.
Material type: Rocks for cutting and polishing.
Material: Chalcedony geodes, chalcedony float.
Level of difficulty: Difficult.
Tools: Shovel.
Vehicle: Utility.
Accommodations: Camping in Coronado National Forest.
Special attractions: None.
Finding the site: Animas is located in the far southwestern corner of the state. Access is from New Mexico Highway 338 south of Animas. From Animas travel about 27 miles south to a fork in the road, take the right fork toward the mountains. Travel west about 7 miles to the Coronado National Forest boundary. Begin looking in washes and all sandy or rocky areas immediately after entering national forest property.
Warning: Take extra water for both your vehicle and for drinking. Take food, and let somebody know where you are going. This site is extremely remote.

Rockhounding: Golf ball- to baseball-sized geodes lined with bubbly white or gray chalcedony make a treasure worth seeking, if you happen to be in this remote corner of the state. Though you are more likely to find broken pieces, full geodes are possible with some careful looking. Once you find a spot littered with scraps, it might be wise to do a little digging in an effort to find geodes hiding below the surface.

There are also some beautiful pieces of loose chalcedony that are similar to that which is found farther east near Hermanas. It is generally milky white or clear. Some pieces contain red splotches or streaks that add immeasurably to their interest. The pieces are generally small, but digging could turn up larger specimens.

If you traveled south from Lordsburg to get here, you may have noticed a group of large buildings to the east of NM 338 near the town Cotton City. From the road it looks like a prison facility. They are actually greenhouses. That does not seem too unusual given the abundant supply of sunshine in this area.

What is unusual, however, is that the greenhouses sit on top of a geothermal area where naturally heated water lies very close to the surface. Enough warmth radiates through the ground to reduce winter heating bills for the greenhouses, melt any snow that falls, and allow for an early growing season for cotton farmers in Cotton City.

Site 64 Chalcedony Geodes Near Animas

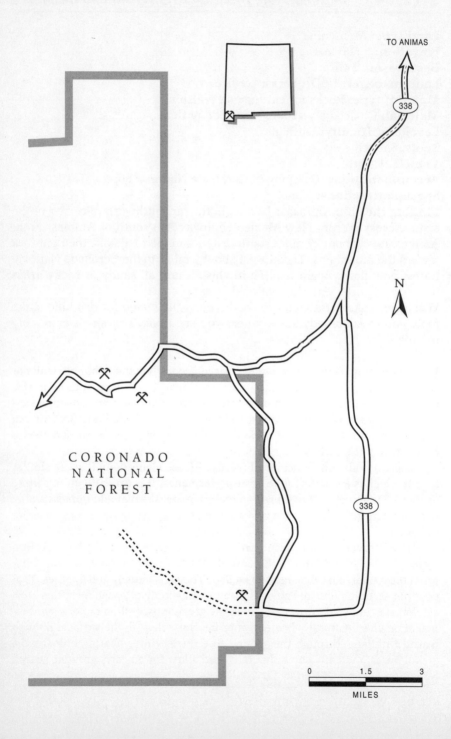

TO ANIMAS

338

N

CORONADO
NATIONAL
FOREST

338

0   1.5   3

MILES

SITE 65 *COPPER MINERALS SOUTH OF LORDSBURG*

Land type: Hills.
Elevation: 4,277 feet.
Best season: Fall.
Land manager: Bureau of Land Management.
Material type: Mineral specimens.
Material: Chrysocolla, azurite, malachite, agate.
Level of difficulty: Moderate.
Tools: Shovel.
Vehicle: Any.
Accommodations: Motels and RV parking in Lordsburg.
Special attractions: None.
For more information: Shakespeare ghost town tours 505-542-9034.
Finding the site: Lordsburg is located on Interstate Highway 10 about 20 miles east of the Arizona border. In Lordsburg take Main Street south out of town. At about 1.35 miles from I-10 the road forks; stay to the left on New Mexico Highway 494. Pass the cemetery, then travel another 0.75 miles to a dirt road leading up a hill. Search in the pit and dumps beyond the crest of the hill.

Rockhounding: This area near the old ghost town of Shakespeare is a prime collecting spot for small samples of copper minerals, especially azurite. It could take a considerable amount of time to find anything worth keeping, but dig a little below the surface and train your eyes on small flecks of color. Some collectors find it useful to use water and a gold pan on dumps like these to help spot the color.

The mining district that is south of Shakespeare is noted for small quantities of silver, copper, gold, lead, zinc, and uranium ores produced in the late 1800s. But notoriety outlives notability. In 1870 a local boom ensued when the richness of silver ore was exaggerated. Then in 1872 promoters deliberately salted an area with diamonds in an attempt to win backing from investors.

Today the town of Shakespeare is renowned as the place where Billy the Kid worked as a dishwasher before he found his calling as an outlaw. Tours of the town are offered on alternate weekends.

SITE 66 *MINERALS NORTH OF LORDSBURG*

Land type: Mountains.
Elevation: 5,400 feet.
Best season: Summer, fall.
Land manager: USDA Forest Service.
Material type: Mineral specimens.

Material: Pyrite, chalcopyrite, allanite, cyrtolite, euxanite, samarskite.
Level of difficulty: Very difficult.
Tools: Shovels, picks, hammers, chisels.
Vehicle: Four-wheel-drive.
Accommodations: RV parking and motels in Lordsburg.
Special attractions: None.
For more information: Gila National Forest Silver City Ranger District 505-538-2771.
Finding the site: Lordsburg is located on Interstate Highway 10 about 20 miles east of the Arizona border. From Lordsburg travel north on U.S. Highway 70. About 1 mile out of town, turn right onto New Mexico Highway 90. Travel about 10.5 miles to Forest Service Road 841. Turn right. The road to the first set of mines and prospect pits is about 2.6 miles down FR 841. Another set of dumps can be found another 1.5 miles farther.

Site 65 Copper Minerals South of Lordsburg & Site 66 Minerals North of Lordsburg

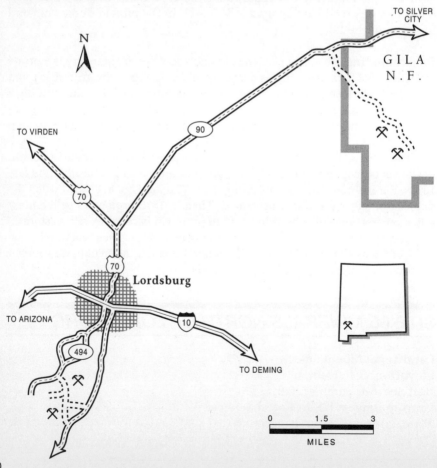

Rockhounding: The Gold Hill Mining District was, unfortunately, one of the least productive districts in this region. Only small amounts of gold, silver, and lead ores were extracted. There are some interesting materials here, however, but you should have excellent background knowledge on these minerals before beginning your search.

Common minerals found here include pyrite, galena, and magnetite, all of which are relatively easy to find throughout the district. Less common are sphalerite (false galena), pyrargyrite (red silver ore), and cerussite. Additionally, the radioactive rare earth minerals of cyrtolite, euxenite, allanite, and samarskite are present here.

This is a rather remote area, and the road is very sandy. Four-wheel-drive is highly recommended. It is very easy to underestimate the difficulty of the road because it looks smooth. Most any vehicle can make the trip, but the hard part is finding a place to turn around. The road is very narrow in places, and where it widens, one false move can put you up to your lug nuts in sand. Do not take any chances.

SITE 67 FIRE AGATE NEAR VIRDEN

Land type: Hills.
Elevation: 4,000 feet.
Best season: Fall.
Land manager: Bureau of Land Management.
Material type: Gemstones, rocks for cutting and polishing.
Material: Agate, fire agate, petrified wood.
Level of difficulty: Very difficult.
Tools: Rake, shovel, water.
Vehicle: Utility.
Accommodations: RV parking and motels in Lordsburg.
Special attractions: None.
Finding the site: Virden is located on New Mexico Highway 92, 2.9 miles east of the Arizona border. From Virden travel west about 1 mile to a dirt road on the right. Search all washes and gullies for the agate.

Rockhounding: The truth here is that this site could very well be the proverbial wild goose chase. But if you have ever seen a really good piece of fire agate, you'll chase this goose and any other that happens along. I did find one tiny sliver with just a hint of color trying to break through, but in the world of fire agate hunters, that one piece is usually validation enough.

Luckily, the other agate is not quite as difficult to find. Colors are principally clear, white, red, and black. Occasional pieces of petrified wood are scattered here as well. The Steeple Rock Mining District lies to the north of here and is accessible from this dirt road, providing road conditions are favorable. Typical finds in that district include lead and copper minerals such as galena, cerussite, azurite, chalcopyrite, malachite, and chrysocolla.

Site 67 Fire Agate Near Virden

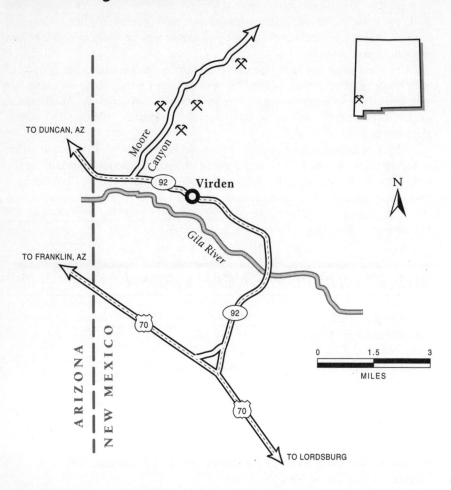

TO DUNCAN, AZ

Moore Canyon

92 **Virden**

Gila River

TO FRANKLIN, AZ

70

92

70

TO LORDSBURG

N

ARIZONA

NEW MEXICO

0   1.5   3

MILES

SITE 68 *PERIDOT AT KILBOURNE HOLE*

Land type: Hills.
Elevation: 4,000 feet.
Best season: Any.
Land manager: Bureau of Land Management.
Material type: Gemstones.
Material: Peridot.
Level of difficulty: Difficult.
Tools: Picks, chisels, hammer.
Vehicle: Four-wheel-drive.
Accommodations: RV parks and motels in El Paso.

Site 68 Peridot at Kilbourne Hole

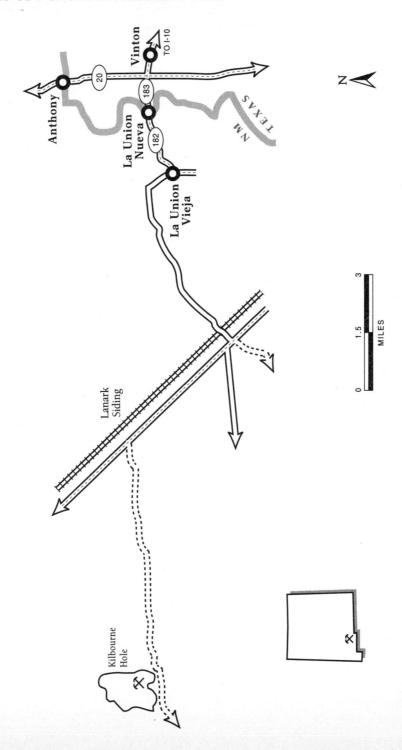

Special attractions: Franklin Mountain garnets in El Paso, Texas.

Finding the site: From either El Paso or Las Cruces, take Interstate Highway 10 to the Vinton/Westway exit. Turn west toward Vinton. Cross the Rio Grande and travel through La Union Nueva on New Mexico Highway 183. At the junction of NM 183 and NM 28, turn right. Travel 0.3 miles to New Mexico 182. Turn left. Travel about 1 mile to NM 273. Turn right. Look for the road heading west at about 0.5 miles. Stay on this dirt road for about 6 miles, until it crosses the railroad tracks. Turn right and follow the tracks for about 4 miles to the railroad siding marker Lanark. Turn left. Travel about 8 miles to Kilbourne Hole.

Finding the Franklin Mountain site: In El Paso take U.S. Highway 54 north to Texas Loop 375 North, which is also known as Trans Mountain Road. Turn east on the Loop. Immediately after beginning the ascent into the mountains there is an area suitable for parking on the right side of the road. The area for collecting is not in the actual road cut facing the highway, but in the exposed mountainside, about 50 feet to the left, facing the parking area. Look for the green of the serpentine, which colors the entire mountainside.

Rockhounding: Okay, okay, so everybody already knows about Kilbourne Hole. Let this just be a reminder that the peridot found out there are some of the best from anywhere. There are still lots of gem quality specimens, some possibly one or two carats in weight.

While you're down that far, and since you're in the mood to hunt for gemstones, you might want to venture into El Paso to look for garnets in the Franklin Mountains. Green-banded serpentine schist studded with garnet makes the trip worthwhile. Some of the garnets are gem quality. Size range is considerable. Most of the crystals are a deep brown grossular variety, but an occasional find of emerald green uvarovite is possible.

Chiseling pieces from the face of the mountain is possible but not necessary, since garnet-studded schist covers the ground near the base of the mountain. The rubble is deep enough, however, that careful digging for the best pieces is a good idea.

While there are no fences restricting access to areas farther down the hillside, away from the road, no access to any area off the immediate roadside is allowed. This is the Fort Bliss artillery range.

SITE 69 *FOSSILS NEAR CLOUDCROFT*

Land type: Mountains.
Elevation: 8,000 feet.
Best season: Summer.
Land manager: USDA Forest Service.
Material type: Fossils in matrix.
Material: Fossils.
Level of difficulty: Difficult.
Tools: Hammer, picks, chisels.
Vehicle: Any.
Accommodations: Motels in Cloudcroft; camping in Lincoln National Forest.
Special attractions: Camping, fishing, and birding.
For more information: Lincoln National Forest 505-682-2551.
Finding the site: Fossils can be found in the limestone beds surrounding this area. Search roadcuts between Cloudcroft and Elk, as well as the area surrounding the national forest campgrounds.

Rockhounding: Hard limestone layers provide the matrix here for Permian-aged marine fossils that include gastropods, cephalopods, and bivalves. Because the area is heavily forested, it takes considerable effort to find suspected samples of rock, then it takes an experienced hand to expose the fossils.

I saw an outstanding example of an ammonite embedded in Permian limestone that had been carefully etched. All it takes is the knowledge that one such specimen was found to provide the incentive to look for your own.

Site 69 Fossils Near Cloudcroft

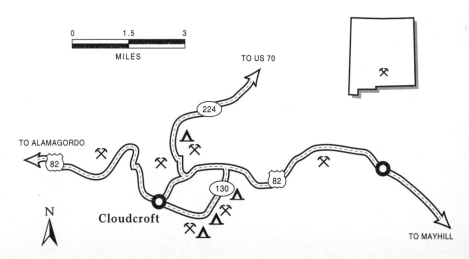

SITE 70 GOLD NEAR RUIDOSO

Land type: Mountains.
Elevation: 6,900 feet.
Best season: Summer.
Land manager: USDA Forest Service.
Material type: Mineral specimen.
Material: Gold.
Level of difficulty: Difficult.
Tools: Gold pan.
Vehicle: Any.
Accommodations: Motels, RV parking in Ruidoso; camping in Lincoln National Forest.
Special attractions: Fishing, hiking, shopping, horse racing.
For more information: Lincoln National Forest 505-257-4095; Bonito Lake 505-827-7882; Ruidoso Downs 505-265-1791.
Finding the site: Ruidoso is located on U.S. Highway 70 at the south end of Lincoln County. From Ruidoso turn north on New Mexico Highway 48 and continue through Alto. About 4.4 miles north of Alto, turn left on NM 37. Travel 1.3 miles, then turn left on Bonito Lake Road. Panning is possible along the Rio Bonito where accessible.

Rockhounding: A rockhounding guide to New Mexico would not be complete without at least one place to pan for gold. Obviously there are numerous other possibilities. It has been said that you can find traces of gold in almost any stream flowing through the state. This site begged to be included in the book because it is easily accessible, offers a strong chance of reward, and it is downright beautiful.

For those who have never undertaken the task of panning for gold, what follows is a beginner's guide. Find a spot along the stream with accessible sand on the bottom. Many swear by sand bars that pile up in front of large rocks. Use your gold pan to scoop up about two handfuls of sand and water. Here's the tricky part that will take some practice. Gently swirl the mixture of sand and water around the pan, occasionally allowing a small amount of water and sand to slosh over the rim of the pan.

The idea here is that the gold, being heavier, will settle to the bottom of the pan and not be swished out with the lighter weight materials. You may need to carefully add more water as the amount in the pan is depleted. Work slowly, keeping an eye on the heavy material in the pan. The more you slosh out, generally the darker the stuff left in the pan will be. This is a really big plus in helping to spot any gold that might be present.

Keep in mind that you are not looking for nuggets here, although that would be nice. The gold will be in the form of tiny particles, commonly known as gold dust. Carefully separate any suspected material, placing it in a small container for the trip home. (Clear film canisters work well for showing the dust to your friends.) Good luck, and don't blow all of your fortune at the racetrack.

Gold panning is a fun pasttime on almost any stream in New Mexico.

Site 70 Gold Near Ruidoso &
Site 71 Minerals in Nogal Mining District

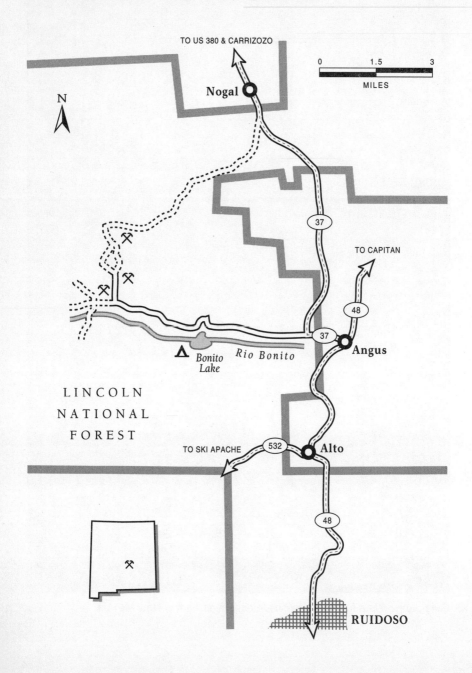

SITE 71 *MINERALS IN NOGAL MINING DISTRICT*

Land type: Mountains.
Elevation: 8,000 feet.
Best season: Summer.
Land manager: USDA Forest Service.
Material type: Mineral specimens.
Material: Barite, pyrite, chrysocolla, galena, sphalerite.
Level of difficulty: Difficult.
Tools: Shovel.
Vehicle: Any.
Accommodations: Motels, cabins, and RV parking in Ruidoso; camping in Lincoln National Forest or at Bonito Lake.
Special attractions: Shopping, museums, and horse racing in Ruidoso.
For more information: Lincoln National Forest 505-257-4095; Bonito Lake 505-827-7882.
Finding the site: The Nogal Mining District is located northwest of Ruidoso. From Ruidoso take New Mexico Highway 48 north through Alto. About 4.4 miles north of Alto, turn left on NM 37. Travel 1.3 miles, then turn left on Bonito Lake Road. Travel 7.1 miles to Forest Service Road 108. Turn right. The mines and dumps continue along this road as it winds up the mountain then back down to the town of Nogal.

Rockhounding: Gold was discovered in the Nogal Mining District in 1865. Though the gold was produced in only small quantities, mainly from placer deposits in Dry Gulch, the district survived on small silver, lead, and copper deposits.

Today the best find on the dumps of the old mines is rock bearing pyrite and quartz veining. Many pieces are capped with a layer of twisted barite crystals. The pickings may be somewhat slim here, but the thick air of history makes this a worthwhile stop if you are in the area. The pine-covered mountains are spectacular. There just aren't many spots in the state that allow rockhounds the multiple pleasures of snooping around in ramshackle mine camps, digging in long forgotten dumps, followed by a day of fishing or watching the ponies run for the money.

SITE 72 *AGATE SOUTH OF ROSWELL*

Land type: Plains.
Elevation: 3,570 feet.
Best season: Any.
Land manager: New Mexico State Highway and Transportation Department.
Material type: Rocks for tumbling.
Material: Agate, jasper, flint.
Level of difficulty: Easy.
Tools: Rake.
Vehicle: Any.
Accommodations: Motels and RV parking in Roswell.
Special attraction: Carlsbad Caverns National Park.
For more information: National park headquarters, 505-785-2232.
Finding the Site: Roswell is located at the junction of U.S. Highway 70/380 and US 285. From Roswell take US 285 south toward Artesia. Travel about 17.5 miles to a rest area near the Rio Felix. Park here and search the nearby roadsides and banks of the river.

Rockhounding: Tiny masterpieces of agate litter the ground like fragments of a broken crystal vase. The principal colors are gray, black, and clear. Many have swirls of red throughout. Look also for warm caramel jasper, red flint, and slivers of petrified wood.

The small tumbling rocks found in this area could be part of the Ogallala gravel mix, the western edge of which lies very near Roswell. The concentration of agate is definitely higher here, however, than that found in most of the formation.

When you're through gathering rocks, a short 76-mile drive south through oil country brings you to one of the premier attractions of the state: Carlsbad Caverns.

The cavern is one of the largest explored caves in the world. Water carved this massive abyss by pouring through fractures in the Capitan Reef limestone. There are other caves in the area, including the famous Lechugilla, which is open only to experienced research groups.

Visitors to the park who wish to experience the thrill of viewing an undeveloped cave will want to make arrangements to tour Slaughter Canyon Cave, formerly called New Cave. It requires a moderately strenuous hike to the entrance and your own flashlight. The town of Carlsbad is also home to the Living Desert State Park, which provides an up-close look at the flora and fauna of this desert region.

Site 72 Agate South of Roswell &
Site 73 Agate and Pecos Diamonds Near Hagerman

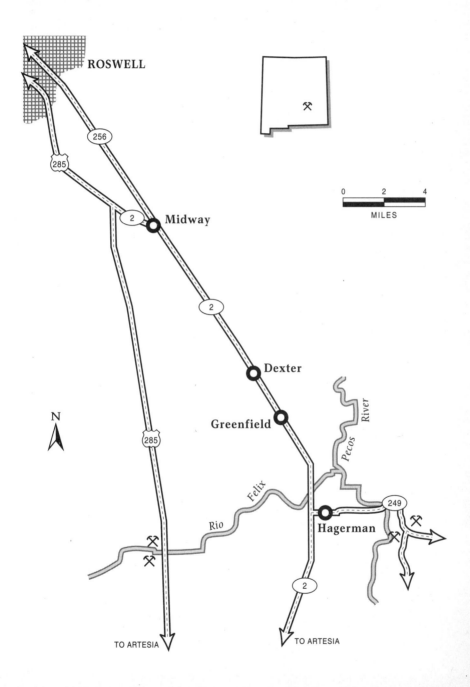

SITE 73 *AGATE AND PECOS DIAMONDS NEAR HAGERMAN*

Land type: Hills.
Elevation: 3,500 feet.
Best season: Any.
Land manager: New Mexico Highway and Transportation Department.
Material type: Rocks for tumbling, mineral specimens.
Material: Agate, jasper, flint, quartz crystals.
Level of difficulty: Moderate to difficult.
Tools: Rake.
Vehicle: Any.
Accommodations: Motels and RV parking in Roswell.
Special attractions: Carlsbad Caverns National Park.
For more information: Carlsbad Caverns National Park 505-785-2232.
Finding the site: Hagerman is located between Roswell and Artesia on New Mexico Highway 2. In Hagerman travel east on New Mexico 242. At about 3.5 miles the road crosses the Pecos River. Good collecting begins alongside the road about 1 mile farther.

Rockhounding: The sandy mesas east of the Pecos River are prime collecting spots for the famed "Pecos Diamonds." Of course they aren't diamonds, but folks in this area are what you would call Near Texans, and as such, are prone to bragging. When the first of these lovely double-terminated quartz crystals was discovered, some rancher probably did a real good job impressing his neighbors with his gems.

Actually reports of the crystals date as far back as 1583. Spanish explorer Don Antonio de Espejo wrote that in some places the desert appeared to be paved with "diamonds." The crystals are quartz replacements of gypsum and sometimes still contain gypsum inclusions.

Today collectors flock to this area and spend hours crawling around in the sand with the rattlesnakes, hoping to find a few of the interesting crystals. They can be elusive, however. While searching for the quartz, don't overlook the very nice array of agate found here. Most pieces are tumbling size only, but if you like the looks of this agate, persistence and sweat could turn up larger specimens.

Though some of the land east of Hagerman is BLM, it is all leased for ranching. If you choose to cross fences, be sure not to disturb the cattle and sheep raised here. One look at the heavy brush growth in this area will be enough to make most collectors refrain from venturing beyond the roadside.

SITE 74 *PECOS DIAMONDS NORTH OF ROSWELL*

Land type: Hills.
Elevation: 3,570 feet.
Best season: Any.
Land manager: New Mexico State Highway and Transportation Department.
Material type: Mineral specimens.
Material: Quartz crystals.
Level of difficulty: Difficult.
Tools: Rake.
Vehicle: Any.
Accommodations: RV Parking and motels in Roswell.
Special attractions: Bitter Lake National Wildlife Refuge 505-622-6755; International UFO Museum and Research Center 505-625-9495.
For more information: Roswell Convention/Visitors Bureau 505-623-5695.
Finding the site: From Roswell travel north on U.S. Highway 285/70. Exit right onto US 70 at the split. Travel northeast about 10.9 miles to the Pecos River. Turn right onto the sandy access road at the east end of the bridge.

Rockhounding: This is just one more chance to look for the famous Pecos Diamonds. Keep in mind that hunting the crystals is a little like hunting arrowheads. There are people who can find them each and every time they look, and there are those who will spend their lives walking right over them.

The best place to look at this site is on the sandy road itself. Keep in mind that they are generally tan colored, like the sand, and usually less than 1 inch long. Don't forget to look for agates and snakes while your eyes are on the ground.

SITE 75 *AGATE AT ACME*

Land type: Hills.
Elevation: 3,570 feet.
Best season: Any.
Land manager: Bureau of Land Management.
Material type: Rocks for cutting, polishing, and tumbling.
Material: Agate, jasper, petrified wood.
Level of difficulty: Easy.
Tools: Rake, shovel.
Vehicle: Any.
Accommodations: Motels and RV parking in Roswell.
Special attractions: None.

Site 74 Pecos Diamonds North of Roswell & Site 75 Agate at Acme

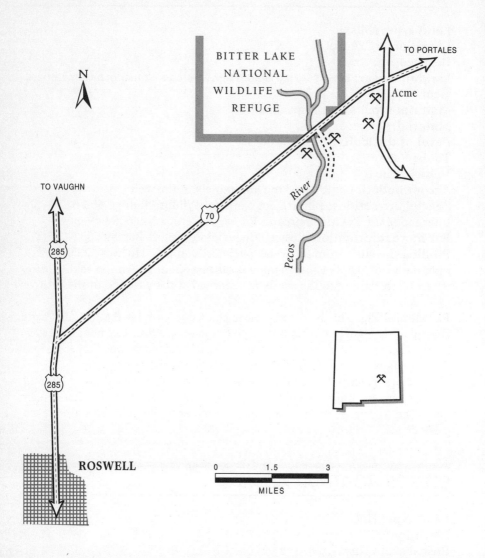

BITTER LAKE
NATIONAL
WILDLIFE
REFUGE

TO PORTALES

Acme

N

TO VAUGHN

285

70

River

Pecos

285

ROSWELL

0   1.5   3

MILES

For more information: Roswell Convention/Visitors Bureau 505-623-5695.
Finding the site: The remains of the town of Acme are located on U.S.
Highway 70 northeast of Roswell. From Roswell travel north on US 285/
70. Exit right onto US 70 at the split. Look for remnants of a large building on the left and a dirt road marked Magdalena Road on the right, about
14 miles from the highway split. Turn right. Collect on and along the road

and in the washes leading to the Pecos River.

Rockhounding: The agate here is much the same as that found throughout the area surrounding Roswell. The color is mostly clear or gray, but many pieces bear bright red streaks and fortification banding. There is an increase in the available sizes at this location, however. Many pieces are large enough for slabbing.

There are also a few small examples of petrified wood here. They are similar to that found in the mix of Ogallala gravel beds that lay from here to the east across the Texas Panhandle.

Finding the best pieces will often take some persistence. A light raking of the surface will often drag up pieces previously overlooked. Larger pieces may also be found by digging (off the road please).

Small agate pebbles ideal for tumbling are plentiful near Rosewell and Acme.

APPENDIX

Bureau of Land Management, P.O. Box 27115, Santa Fe, New Mexico 87502-7115, 505-438-7400. Ask for free Recreation and Heritage Guide or send $4.00 for a detailed Federal Land Ownership Map.

Carson National Forest, P.O. Box 558, Taos, New Mexico 87571, 505-758-6288.

Cibola National Forest, 2113 Osuna Road, N.E., Albuquerque, New Mexico 87113-1001, 505-761-4650.

Gila National Forest, 2610 North Silver Street, Silver City, New Mexico 88061, 505-388-8201.

Lincoln National Forest, 1101 New York, Alamagordo, New Mexico 88310-6992, 505-437-6030.

Santa Fe National Forest, P.O. Box 1689, Santa Fe, New Mexico 87504, 505-988-6940.

U.S. Geological Survey, Distribution Section Federal Center, Building 41, Denver, Colorado 80225, 303-234-3832.

GLOSSARY

Agate: A banded, or variegated chalcedony.

Agatized: Impregnated with silicon dioxide, producing a secondary material that is banded or variegated.

Alabaster: A very fine-grained variety of gypsum.

Amazonite: Light blue green gemstone variety of microcline orthoclase.

Azurite: Copper carbonate; dark blue, usually associated with malachite.

Barite: Barium sulfate; crystals often tabular or prismatic.

Basalt: Most common of the volcanic igneous rocks, also known as scoria and the Hawaiian name of "aa."

Beryl: Beryllium aluminum silicate; gemstone varieties include emerald, aquamarine, morganite.

Botryoidal: Bumpy; resembling a bunch of grapes.

Bouquet Agate: Multi-colored agate bearing flower-like inclusions.

Brachiopods: Members of a small phylum of marine animals with bivalve shells similar to oysters and clams.

Bryozoans: Members of the phylum Bryozoa of aquatic animals, with a tubular body and generally with a sponge-like texture.

Cabbing: The act of creating a cabochon.

Cabochon: A stone shaped into a convex curve and polished but unfaceted.

Calcite: Calcium carbonate; often in clear crystals.

Carnelian: A dark red to orange translucent variety of chalcedony.

Carnotite: Yellow uranium ore.

Casting: A fossil created when the impression left by a living plant or animal is filled with another material.

Cephalopod: A member of the marine animal class Cephalopoda; includes nautiluses and ammonites.

Chalcedony: A microcrystalline form of quartz (silicon dioxide); varieties include agate, carnelian, onyx, flint, jasper, chrysoprase, and heliotrope.

Chalcopyrite: Copper iron sulfide; similar to pyrite in appearance, but tarnishes iridescent blue or purple; also known as "peacock ore."

Chrysocolla: Copper silicate; green to blue green; microcrystalline; frequently associated with malachite, azurite, and limonite.

Chert: A sedimentary rock composed chiefly of silicon dioxide; often confused with chalcedony; contains impurities, making it opaque, slightly dull, and less colorful; some flints are actually chert, rather than the purer chalcedony.

Crinoid: A member of the large aquatic animal class Crinoidea; consists of tubular bodies composed of stacked "buttons," crowned by five or more feathery arms.

Dendrites: Tree-like inclusions of one mineral in another.

Dike: A vertical crack in a rock layer filled with igneous matter.

Dolomite: Calcium magnesium carbonate; possible in both crystalline and granular varieties.

Dremel tools: A brand of small motorized power tools with interchangeable bits.

Echinoids: Sea urchins and sand dollars; members of the marine animal class Echinoidea.

Feldspar: Any of a group of rock-forming silicate minerals.

Fire agate: Agate that iridesces from within.

Flint: An opaque variety of chalcedony or chert, in colors including gray, black, brown, white, or red.

Float: Rock material found in a location other than that in which it originally formed.

Fluorescent: Luminescent in the presence of a stimulus, usually ultraviolet light.

Fluorite: Calcium fluoride; purple, blue, green blue, clear, yellow, brown, rose red crystals, often cubic.

Fortification agate: Multi-colored agate bearing swirls or banding of alternating colors that follow the shape of the rock.

Fossil: The remains or impressions of once-living things from the remote geological past.

Gad: A pointed tool used for loosening or breaking rock.

Galena: Lead sulfide; presenting cubic cleavage.

Gastropod: A member of the largest class of mollusks, Gastropoda, including snails.

Geode: A hollow rock nodule often lined with crystals.

Granite: Medium- to fine-grained rock normally composed of feldspar, quartz, and mica.

Grossular: A variety of garnet; can be colorless, white, yellow, pink, green or brown.

Hematite: Iron oxide; can occur in massive forms, as black crystals or as a red powder.

Igneous: Rock formed by the cooling of molten of volcanic matter.

Ilmenite: Iron titanium oxide; black or brownish black; weakly magnetic.

Inclusion: One mineral enclosed within another.

Jasper: A variegated, mottled, opaque form of chalcedony in colors of red, yellow, or brown.

Labradorite: Multi-colored variety of feldspar.

Lepidolite: Lithium ore in the mica group.

Limonite: A mixture of hydrous iron oxides.

Lineation: Arrangement in lines.

Lower Cretaceous: The first half of the Cretaceous Period, 144 million to 66 million years ago.

Lower Tertiary: The first half of the Tertiary Period, 66 million to 37 million years ago.

Magnetite: Iron oxide, dark and metallic, heavily magnetic.

Malachite: Basic copper carbonate; emerald to grass green with concentric color banding.

Manganite: Manganese oxide; steel gray to black crystals.

Matrix: The dirt or rock in which a fossil or mineral is embedded.

Metamorphic: Rocks that have undergone a complete change in character or chemical make-up due to extreme heat, pressure, or both.

Mica: Any of a group of silicate minerals formed in thin sheets.

Microcrystalline: Having crystals visible only through a microscope.

Mohs scale: A scale of hardness for rating minerals, one (talc) being the softest, and ten (diamond) the hardest.

Molybdenite: Molybdenum sulfide; blue gray, metallic.

Muscovite: Form of mica.

Obsidian: Gray to black volcanic glass.

Onyx: Banded, opaque variety of chalcedony, usually in colors of red, white, and golden tan.

Opal: An amorphous form of hydrous silica, usually with a deep play of color (fire).

Orthoclase: Potassium aluminum silicate in the group commonly known as feldspar.

Paleocene: Epoch in the Tertiary Period, 66 million to 58 million years ago.

Pegmatite: Course-grained variety of granite.

Pennsylvanian: Period in the Paleozoic Era, 320 million to 286 million years ago.

Plume agate: A variety of agate characterized by single-color inclusions of tree-like formations.

Pom Pom agate: An agate variety with colorful circles or balls of another color.

Porphyry: Fine-grained igneous rock in which larger crystals are encased.

Pseudomorphs: A mineral that has taken the outward crystal formation of another mineral.

Pyrite: Iron disulfide; commonly known as "fool's gold."

Quartzite: Rock in which quartz is the predominate mineral.

Schist: Medium- to coarse-grained, metamorphic rock with prominent parallel mineral orientation.

Sedimentary: Rock formed by the compaction and cementation of fragments of other rocks or living creatures or by the precipitation of material from a solution.

Selenite: Colorless, transparent gypsum crystals.

Slag: Waste matter obtained when ore is smelted.

Smithsonite: Zinc carbonate; named for James Smithson who founded the Smithsonian Institution.

Smoky quartz: Pale brown to black variety of quartz.

Snowflake obsidian: Black obsidian bearing delicate snowflake-like inclusions.

Specific gravity: Relative weight of any substance given numbers comparing the weight of one substance to that of an equal volume of water; example: a mineral with a specific gravity of two is twice as heavy as water.

Staurolite: Iron and aluminum silicate often found in twinned crystals.

Streak plate: A white, unglazed tile used to identify minerals based on the color they leave when scraped on the tile.

Tertiary: Period of the Cenozoic Era, 66 million to 2 million years ago.

Tourmaline: A group of boron silicate minerals that include the gemstones indicolite, dravite, and the multi-colored watermelon tourmaline.

Trilobite: A member of the extinct class of marine arthropods Trilobita.

Thunder eggs: Solid round agate nodules appearing like geodes on the exterior, but are not hollow.

Tuff: Rock formed from compacted volcanic ash and cinders.

Turritella: Genus of long, slender snails.

Upper Cretaceous: The second half of the Cretaceous Period, 144 million to 66 million years ago.

Uvarovite: Emerald green variety of garnet.

Valles Caldera: Term used to describe the crater left behind after a volcano has exploded, then collapsed in upon itself; namesake caldera is found in the Jemez Mountains, and both "Jemez" and "Valles" are used to describe the crater there.

Vein: A mineral deposit clearly separated from the rock around it.

INDEX

copper 108, 124, 129
Coronado National Forest 127
Cotton City, New Mexico 127
coyote 10
Coyote, New Mexico 18, 19, 22
crinoid stems 38
Cuba, New Mexico 15, 16, 18, 19
cuprite 82
cyrtolite 130, 131

D

Deming, New Mexico 4, 5, 115, 116, 119,
    120, 123
dinosaur fossils 24
Dixon, New Mexico 48

E

Eagle Nest, New Mexico 57
El Paso, Texas 134
Elizabethtown Ghost Town 57
Elk, New Mexico 135
Española, New Mexico 24, 26
euxanite 130
euxenite 131

F

Farmington, New Mexico 4
Fenton Lake 18
flint 63, 65, 67, 68, 140, 142
fluorite 4, 37, 38, 60, 70, *71*, 72, 115, 116
Forks Campground 103
fossils 12, 37, 38, 58, 63, 64, *65*, 67, 68,
    111, 135. *See also* specific fossil
    names
Franklin Mountains 134

G

gabbro 58
galena 60, 70, 74, 80, 131, 139
Galisteo, New Mexico 62
Gallina, New Mexico 18, 19
garnet 27, 28, 38, 42, 50, 52, 134
gastropods 64, 135
geodes 27
Gila Cliff Dwellings National Monument
    102, 103
Gila National Forest 5, 84, 86, 87, 89, 90,
    100, 102, 103, 109, 111
Gila River *101*, 102
gold 37, 38, 50, 57, 118, 129, 136
Gold Hill Mining District 131

granite
graphic 57
   pegmatic 58
Grants, New Mexico 41, 42, 44, 45
Grapevine Campground 100, 102, 103
gypsum 18, 44, 142

H

Hagerman, New Mexico 142
Hanover, New Mexico 103, 104
Hansonberg Mining District 72
Harding Pegmatite Mine 48, *49*
Hatch, New Mexico 111, 113
hematite 19, 20, 37, 38, 65, 80
hemimorphite 108, 109
Hermanas, New Mexico 2, 121
Hobbs, New Mexico 5

I

Ice Caves 42
ilmenite 27, 28

J

jarosite 80
jasper 15, 23, 27, 35, 62, 63, 65, 67, 68,
    93, 110, 111, 115, 120, 140, 142, 143
Jemez Indian Reservation 15, 30
Jemez Springs, New Mexico 18, 29, 30,
    31, 32
Jemez Valley 32, 35
Jones Camp Iron Mines 74, *75*, 76

K

Kelly Mine 5, *6*, 81, 82, *83*
Kelly Mining District 72
Kilbourne Hole 132, 134
Kingston Mines 108, 109
Kingston, New Mexico 109

L

La Cueva, New Mexico 31
La Luz Mine 38
La Luz Trail 38
La Madera, New Mexico 27
labradorite 95, 96
Las Cruces, New Mexico 4, 134
Las Vegas, New Mexico 64
lava flow 76
lead 129
Lechugilla Cave 140
lepidolite 48, 57

linarite 70, 72
Lincoln National Forest 135, 136
Living Desert State Park 140
Lobo Canyon 44
Logan, New Mexico 67
Lordsburg, New Mexico 129, 130
Los Cerrillos, New Mexico 63
Luna, New Mexico 89, 90, 91, 92

M
Magdalena, New Mexico 82
magnetite 74, 131
malachite 16, 18, 37, 38, 81, 82, 103, 105, 129, 131
Malpais Lava Beds 42
manganese oxides 76, 77, 78, 79, 108, 109, 116
manganite 108
McKinley County 47
mica books 28
mica schist 52
microcline 48
mimetite 80
Mogollon, New Mexico 97, 98
mollusks 58
molybdenite 52
monzonite 54
Mount Taylor 42, 44
Mule Creek 100
muscovite 27
    rose 48, 55, *56*

N
Navajo Reservation 47
New Mexico Institute of Mining and Technology 70, 82
New Mexico Mining Museum 41, 42, 44, 45
New Mexico Museum of Natural History 32, 35, 36
Nogal Mining District 139

O
obsidian 4, 29, 30, 32, 34, *41*, 42, 43, 100
    snowflake 30, *32*
Oglalla Formation 67
Ojo Caliente, New Mexico 27
opal 65, 67, 114
orthoclase 37, 38
    crystals 54

P
Palisades, the 58
Paliza Campground 30
Pancho Villa State Park 122
Patterson Peak 84
Pecos Diamonds 142, 143
Pecos National Historical Park 60
Pecos, New Mexico 60
Pecos River 142
pegmatite 28
peridot 132, 134
Petaca Mine Dumps 27, 28
Petaca, New Mexico 27
petrified wood 4, 12, 15, *17*, 35, 36, 39, *40*, 45, 47, 52, 62, 65, 67, 68, 69, 70, 103, 111, 113, 114, 131, 140, 143, 145
    agatized 70
    opalized 70
Pilar, New Mexico 50
piñon tree 2
Playas, New Mexico 124
Ponderosa, New Mexico 29, 30
porphyry 54
Portales, New Mexico 5
psilomelane 78, 79, 80, 108, 109, 115, 116, 118
Pueblo Park 89, 96
pyrargyrite 131
pyrite 60, 79, 80, 81, 82, 130, 131, 139
pyrolusite 78

Q
quartz 26, 27, 48, 50, 70, 81, 91, *92*, 97
    citrine 82
    crystals 90, 92, 142, 143
    drusy 108, 109
    rose 80
    smoky 27, 28, 82
quartzite 65
Quay County 67
Quemado, New Mexico 5
Questa Molybdenum Mines 52

R
raccoon 9–10
Rancho Grande Estates, New Mexico 90
Raton, New Mexico 58
Red Hill, New Mexico 93, 95
Red River, New Mexico 54
Reserve, New Mexico 87

ABOUT THE AUTHOR

Melinda Crow is a free-lance journalist who writes to learn. Though she was born in Amarillo, Texas, her father moved to Albuquerque in 1969, affording her the opportunity of dual residency in Texas and New Mexico.

This is her second book in the *Rockhound's Guide* series, and her work has appeared in magazines such as *Texas Highways, National Gardening, 3-2-1 Contact, Parenting,* and *Family Fun*. Family-oriented travel and activity writing is her specialty.

She is a certified Master Gardener. With the help of her husband Gary and daughter Alyssa, she is creating a native plant garden that showcases many of her rock treasures.

*Melinda
Crow*

FALCON GUIDES | *Perfect for every outdoor adventure!*

ANGLER'S GUIDES
Angler's Guide to Alaska
Angler's Guide to Florida
Angler's Guide to Montana

BACKCOUNTRY HORSEMAN'S GUIDES
Backcountry Horseman's Guide to Washington
Backcountry Horseman's Guide to Montana

FLOATER'S GUIDES
Floater's Guide to Colorado
Floater's Guide to Missouri
Floater's Guide to Montana

HIKER'S GUIDES
Hiker's Guide to Alaska
Hiker's Guide to Alberta
Hiker's Guide to Arizona
Hiker's Guide to California
Hiker's Guide to Colorado
Hiker's Guide to Florida
Hiker's Guide to Georgia
Hiker's Guide to Hot Springs
   in the Pacific Northwest
Hiker's Guide to Idaho
Hiker's Guide to Montana
Hiker's Guide to Montana's
   Continental Divide Trail
Hiker's Guide to Maine
Hiker's Guide to Nevada
Hiker's Guide to New Hampshire
Hiker's Guide to New Mexico
Hiker's Guide to Oregon
Hiker's Guide to Texas

Hiker's Guide to Utah
Hiker's Guide to Virginia
Hiker's Guide to Washington
Hiker's Guide to Wyoming
Trail Guide to Glacier/Waterton National Parks
Trail Guide to the Beartooths
Trail of the Great Bear
Trail Guide to Northern Arizona
Trail Guide to Bob Marshall Country
Trail Guide to Olympic National Park

ROCK CLIMBER'S GUIDES
Rock Climber's Guide to Colorado
Rock Climber's Guide to Montana

MOUNTAIN BIKER'S GUIDES
Mountain Biker's Guide to Arizona
Mountain Biker's Guide to Central Appalachia
Mountain Biker's Guide to Colorado
Mountain Biker's Guide to Ozarks
Mountain Biker's Guide to New Mexico
Mountain Biker's Guide to Northern New England
Mountain Biker's Guide to the Northern Rockies
Mountain Biker's Guide to the Pacific Northwest
Mountain Biker's Guide to the Southeast
Mountain Biker's Guide to Southern New England
Mountain Biker's Guide to Northern California/
   Nevada
Mountain Biker's Guide to Southern California
Mountain Biker's Guide to the Great Lakes States
Mountain Biker's Guide to Utah
Mountain Biker's Guide to the Midwest

Wild Country Companion

FALCON GUIDES

THE WATCHABLE WILDLIFE SERIES
Arizona Wildlife Viewing Guide
California Wildlife Viewing Guide
Colorado Wildlife Viewing Guide
Florida Wildlife Viewing Guide
Idaho Wildlife Viewing Guide
Indiana Wildlife Viewing Guide
Kentucky Wildlife Viewing Guide
Montana Wildlife Viewing Guide
Nevada Wildlife Viewing Guide
New Mexico Wildlife Viewing Guide
North Carolina Wildlife Viewing Guide
North Dakota Wildlife Viewing Guide
Oregon Wildlife Viewing Guide
Tennessee Wildlife Viewing Guide
Texas Wildlife Viewing Guide
Utah Wildlife Viewing Guide
Vermont Wildlife Viewing Guide
Virginia Wildlife Viewing Guide
Washington Wildlife Viewing Guide
Wisconsin Wildlife Viewing Guide

BIRDER'S GUIDES
Birder's Guide to Arizona
Birder's Guide to Montana

SCENIC DRIVING GUIDES
Scenic Byways
Scenic Byways II
Back Country Byways
Arizona Scenic Drives
California Scenic Drives
Colorado Scenic Drives
Montana Scenic Drives
New Mexico Scenic Drives
Oregon Scenic Drives
Texas Scenic Drives
Traveler's Guide to the Lewis & Clark Trail
Traveler's Guide to the Oregon Trail
Traveler's Guide to the Pony Express Trail

ROCKHOUND'S GUIDES
Rockhound's Guide to Arizona
Rockhound's Guide to California
Rockhound's Guide to Colorado
Rockhound's Guide to Montana
Rockhound's Guide to New Mexico
Rockhound's Guide to Texas

■ *To order any of these books, or to request an expanded list of available titles, including guides for viewing wildlife, birding, scenic driving, or rockhounding, please call 1-800-582-2665, or write to Falcon, PO Box 1718, Helena, MT 59624.*